DATE DUE

Red Velvet Lover's

COOKBOOK

Best-Ever Recipes for Everything Red Velvet,
with More than 50 Scrumptious Sweets and Treats

DEBORAH HARROUN

The Harvard Common Press
BOSTON, MASSACHUSETTS

The Harvard Common Press

www.harvardcommonpress.com

Printed in China

Printed on acid-free paper

Library of Congress Cataloging-in-Publication Data

Harroun, Deborah.

Red velvet lover's cookbook : best-ever recipes for everything red velvet, with more
than 50 scrumptious sweets and treats / Deborah Harroun.

pages cm

Includes index.

ISBN 978-1-55832-834-1 (alk. paper)

1. Cake. I. Title.

TX771.H335 2014

641.86'53--dc23

2014001626

Special bulk-order discounts are available on this and other Harvard Common Press books.
Companies and organizations may purchase books for premiums or resale, or may
arrange a custom edition, by contacting the Marketing Director at the website above.

Book design by Virginia Downes

Photographs by Deborah Harroun

10 9 8 7 6 5 4 3 2 1

For Josh, Abbi, Easton, and Camden.
Thank you for being my inspiration.

Contents

Introduction

I grew up in a small town in New Mexico, so red velvet cake wasn't part of my childhood. In fact, I think the first time I had even heard of it was while watching the movie *Steel Magnolias*. I remember looking at the red velvet armadillo cake covered in gray icing in the famous wedding scene and trying to decide if I was intrigued or appalled. Well, as it turns out, I was intrigued, because from that point on, I couldn't wait to try this cake.

It wasn't until I was grown and had moved away from home that I actually had my first taste of red velvet. From that moment, I was hooked!

So what exactly *is* red velvet?

As a lover of red velvet, I get asked this question quite often. And honestly, it's a hard one to answer. Some will say that it is a chocolate cake that is dyed red. I disagree. Red velvet has only a light cocoa flavor. In fact, I've heard it said that the only reason cocoa is used in the cake is that it masks the flavor of the red food coloring. I say that a red velvet cake or cupcakes taste like butter cake with just a hint of cocoa. It may be a hard flavor to describe, but once you've had it, you probably won't forget it!

I originally thought that serving red velvet would be a great way to mark Valentine's Day. After all, red is the color of love, right? It *is* perfect for that holiday, but the more I made, the more I realized that Valentine's Day is not the only celebration worthy of red velvet. The Fourth of July, Christmas, even Halloween (blood red, anyone?) are all perfect times to pull out red velvet recipes. But really, you don't need a special occasion to indulge in a little red velvet!

The Story of Red Velvet

The history of red velvet is not black and white. In fact, it is quite mysterious and shrouded in controversy. There are many stories about how red velvet came to be, where it actually originated, and who was the first to make it. There are even controversies over what kind of frosting goes on a traditional red velvet cake and what should be used to color the cake.

One of the most famous red velvet stories begins at the Waldorf-Astoria. It is said that the restaurant at this New York City hotel was the first to serve red velvet cake as we know it today. According to legend, a woman visited the Waldorf-Astoria, tried the cake, and fell in love. She wrote a letter to the hotel, asking if the chef would send her the recipe. The hotel did send her the recipe—along with a bill for $350. In retaliation, she made copies of the recipe and distributed them high and low. While this story is entertaining, I doubt its authenticity; the same basic urban myth has also circulated about cookie recipes from Neiman Marcus and Mrs. Fields.

Another story claims that the recipe originated in Canada at the restaurant and bakery in Eaton's department store. In the 1940s and '50s, the store promoted the cake as an Eaton's original, invented by the wife of the owner of the store, Lady Eaton.

In the 1950s, a woman in Pennsylvania sent a recipe for Village Inn Red Cake to a newspaper recipe contest and won $5. And yet another story says the cake was created by Betty Adams during the Great Depression. Adams Extract, based in Texas, was one of the first companies to sell food coloring. To market its red food coloring, the company printed the recipe for red velvet cake on tear-off cards that were placed by the food coloring on grocery store shelves. Adams claims its recipe is the one that popularized today's red velvet, which gets its bright red color from food coloring.

The origin stories of red velvet go on and on. But if you go back in time, there are mentions of so-called velvet cakes in cookbooks from as early as the late 1800s. It is assumed that "velvet" referred to the fine, moist, tender crumb of the cake. There are mentions of a "red devil's food cake" in books from the 1920s, but many people speculate that the "red" wasn't for the color of the cake but because it was made from brown sugar, which was sometimes called "red" sugar back then. Some say that the natural cocoa powder used back then, combined with the vinegar and buttermilk, caused a chemical reaction that turned the cake a shade of red. Scientists debate this theory, though, saying that the amount of anthocyanins (red vegetable pigments) in the cocoa would have been too small to create a noticeable change in color.

More controversy swirls around the question of frosting for a red velvet cake. Most folks think cream cheese frosting is the only way to go. But many accounts suggest that a boiled frosting is traditional for a red velvet cake. While I am a sucker for cream cheese frosting—and prefer it on my red velvet cupcakes—I am a recent convert to using boiled frosting on my red velvet cake. It's a simple frosting that really lets the red velvet cake shine.

Regardless of its history, one thing is for sure. Red velvet is on the rise. And that armadillo cake in *Steel Magnolias* has been credited for bringing red velvet back into the spotlight. Today, it would be hard to find a cupcake bakery that doesn't feature a red velvet cupcake on its menu. Many of them say red velvet is their most popular flavor.

Red velvet also goes way beyond cakes and cupcakes. There are dozens of variations on the bright red concoction. Although some of these recipes may not have that famous "velvet" texture, they still sport the things that make red velvet distinctive—the hint of cocoa and the bright red color.

Dutch-Process Cocoa vs. Natural Cocoa Powder

There are two main types of unsweetened cocoa powder: Dutch process and natural. Dutch-process cocoa has been treated to neutralize its acidity. It is usually darker in color than natural cocoa powder, and baking powder is used in most recipes that call for Dutch-process cocoa; this type of cocoa should not be used with baking soda, which requires acidity to work properly. Natural cocoa powder—the cocoa powder called for in the recipes in this book—is made up of cocoa beans that have been simply roasted and then pulverized into powder. It's the kind typically found on grocery store shelves, including such brands as Hershey's and Nestlé.

Natural Substitutes

If you love red velvet, but not the idea of all that food coloring, there are some substitutes.

If you go back to the days of World War II, there are accounts of red velvet cakes made with beets—claiming the beets were replacing either cocoa or sugar that had been rationed. Today, beets are often used as a substitute for red food coloring, but I don't care for the flavor they impart. Plus, there is some chemistry involved in making a red velvet cake with beets; the pH balance must be just right, or the cake will not be red at all. You can purchase or make your own beetroot powder, which is probably a better choice than using beets since the powder doesn't add excess moisture to your recipes.

You can also add other naturally red foods—berries, pomegranates, cranberries—in place of food coloring. I have even seen hibiscus flowers used. You will get varying degrees of the red color, and these ingredients will affect the recipe's flavor, but they are all ways to color foods naturally.

You can also purchase commercial all-natural, vegetable-based food dyes. They are often harder to find and more expensive, and they don't produce bright, vibrant colors, but they are all-natural options. Natural foods stores will carry them, or you can purchase them online through companies like India Tree (indiatree.com) or Natures Flavors (naturesflavors.com).

All of the recipes in this cookbook were tested with the red food coloring you can find on any grocery-store shelf. If you would like to use one of the all-natural substitutes, you may need to play with the quantities of coloring needed.

THE
Basics

The Ultimate Red Velvet Cake

Go big or go home, right? When I think of red velvet, I think impressive. And a two-layer cake just isn't a showstopper. So I decided to go all the way, with four full layers. For this recipe, I use boiled frosting, which I think lets the red velvet truly shine. If you are a cream cheese person, feel free to swap that in, but you should at least try this once with boiled frosting. You won't be sorry!

MAKES ONE 4-LAYER 9-INCH CAKE

4½ cups all-purpose flour
¼ cup natural unsweetened cocoa powder
2 teaspoons table salt
1 cup (2 sticks) unsalted butter, softened
3 cups sugar
4 large eggs
2 cups buttermilk
3 ounces (6 tablespoons) red liquid food coloring
2 teaspoons vanilla extract
2 teaspoons distilled white vinegar
2 teaspoons baking soda
2 batches of Boiled Frosting (page 16)
1½ cups toasted pecans, coarsely chopped

1. Position oven racks in the upper and lower thirds of the oven and preheat the oven to 350°F. Line four 9-inch cake pans with parchment paper. Spray the pans and the parchment paper with nonstick cooking spray.

2. Whisk the flour, cocoa, and salt in a bowl to combine.

3. Beat the butter and sugar in a large bowl with an electric mixer on medium speed until fluffy, about 5 minutes. Add the eggs one at a time, beating for 30 seconds and scraping down the sides of the bowl after each addition. Add the dry ingredients and the buttermilk to the creamed butter and sugar in two or three alternating additions, mixing until combined. Mix in the red food coloring and the vanilla.

4. Combine the vinegar and baking soda in a small bowl (it will bubble up). Fold into the cake batter. Divide the batter evenly among the four cake pans. Bake until the cakes spring back when lightly touched, 30 to 35 minutes. Let the cakes cool for 10 minutes in the pans, then turn out and cool completely on a rack.

5. Spread a small dollop of frosting on a cake plate. Place one cake layer on it and use an offset spatula to spread a layer of frosting to the edges of the cake. Add another cake layer, and spread another layer of frosting on top.

RECIPE CONTINUES

Continue with the remaining cake layers. Cover the top and sides of the cake with a thin coating of frosting. Let this crumb coat harden for a few minutes, then use the rest of the frosting to cover the top and sides of the cake. If desired, use the back of a spoon to make mountains and valleys in the frosting on top of the cake, or use a knife to make swirls. Gently press the pecans into the sides of the cake.

THE ULTIMATE RED VELVET CAKE, *variation*

Red Velvet Tres Leches Cake

Halve the ingredients and prepare the Velvet Cake. Spread the batter in a 9 x 13-inch baking dish sprayed with nonstick cooking spray. Bake in the middle of an oven preheated to 350°F until the cake springs back when touched, 35 to 40 minutes.

Meanwhile, in a medium bowl, combine 14 ounces sweetened condensed milk, 12 ounces evaporated milk, and ½ cup heavy cream.

When the cake comes out of the oven, poke the top of the cake all over with the handle of a wooden spoon and pour the milk mixture over the cake. Let the cake cool completely in the dish.

Mix 1 (16-ounce) container of whipped topping with 8 ounces of softened cream cheese. Spread over the top of the cake and sprinkle with mini chocolate chips.

OPPOSITE:
The Ultimate Red Velvet Cake

The Best Red Velvet Cupcakes

The red velvet cupcake is probably the best-known red velvet dessert out there. I'll admit that I'm pretty picky when it comes to red velvet cupcakes. They shouldn't contain too much cocoa, the frosting has to be something a little special, and—above all—they must be moist. The biggest difference between my red velvet cake and my red velvet cupcake is that I make the cupcakes with oil instead of butter. This ensures that the cupcake stays moist and has that perfect red velvet texture.

I like my cupcakes piled high with cream cheese frosting, but you really can't go wrong with any of the frosting recipes later in this chapter. MAKES 24

2¼ cups all-purpose flour
1 teaspoon table salt
1 tablespoon natural unsweetened cocoa powder
1½ cups sugar
1 cup vegetable oil
2 large eggs
3 tablespoons red liquid food coloring
1 cup buttermilk
1½ teaspoons vanilla extract
1 teaspoon distilled white vinegar
1 teaspoon baking soda
1 batch of Cream Cheese Frosting (page 16)

1. Set a rack in the center position and preheat the oven to 350°F. Line two 12-cavity muffin tins with paper liners.

2. Whisk the flour, salt, and cocoa in a bowl to combine.

3. Beat the sugar and oil in a large bowl with an electric mixer. Add the eggs, one at a time, beating for 30 seconds and scraping down the sides of the bowl after each addition. Mix in the red food coloring.

4. Add the dry ingredients and the buttermilk to the sugar mixture in two or three alternating additions, mixing until combined. Stir in the vanilla. Combine the vinegar and baking soda in a small bowl (it will bubble up). Fold into the batter.

5. Fill each paper liner about two-thirds full with batter. Bake until a tester inserted in the center of a cupcake comes out clean, about 18 minutes. Cool completely on a rack.

6. Frost cooled cupcakes with cream cheese frosting.

Boiled Frosting

Many Southerners believe this is the only way to go when it comes to frosting a red velvet cake. Although I love cream cheese frosting, I now have a new passion for this frosting on my red velvet cake. Call me a convert.

6 tablespoons all-purpose flour
¾ teaspoon table salt
1½ cups whole milk
1½ cups (3 sticks) unsalted butter, softened
1½ cups sugar
2 teaspoons vanilla extract

1. Combine the flour, salt and ½ cup of the milk in a saucepan and whisk until smooth, then whisk in the remaining 1 cup milk. Cook over medium heat until thickened, whisking occasionally. Remove from the heat and cool completely.

2. Beat the butter and sugar in a large bowl with an electric mixer until light and fluffy. Add the vanilla and the cooled milk mixture. Beat until light and fluffy and no longer grainy. Spread on cooled cake or cupcakes. The frosting can be stored in the refrigerator. Bring to room temperature and beat again before using.

Cream Cheese Frosting

Cream cheese frosting is what most of us associate with red velvet, and this is my all-time favorite cream cheese frosting recipe. The sour cream may seem like an odd addition, but it gives this frosting something a little bit special that will leave people asking what makes it taste so good.

12 ounces cream cheese, softened
12 tablespoons (1½ sticks) unsalted butter, softened
1¾ cups plus 1 tablespoon confectioners' sugar
2 tablespoons sour cream
¾ teaspoon vanilla extract

Beat the cream cheese and butter in a large bowl with an electric mixer until light and fluffy. Gradually beat in the confectioners' sugar. Beat in the sour cream and vanilla. Spread on cooled cake or cupcakes. The frosting can be stored in the refrigerator. Bring to room temperature and beat again before using.

White Chocolate Cream Cheese Frosting

Rich and creamy, this frosting is made extra special by the addition of melted white chocolate. The better the quality of the white chocolate, the better it will incorporate into the frosting. So don't skimp!

8 ounces cream cheese, softened
8 tablespoons (1 stick) unsalted butter, softened
2 ounces white chocolate, melted and cooled
3 cups confectioners' sugar
1 teaspoon vanilla extract

Beat the cream cheese and butter in a large bowl with an electric mixer until light and fluffy. Beat in the white chocolate. Gradually beat in the confectioners' sugar. Beat in the vanilla. Spread on cooled cake or cupcakes. The frosting can be stored in the refrigerator. Bring to room temperature and beat again before using.

Marshmallow Cream Cheese Frosting

Although the flavor in this frosting doesn't scream marshmallow, the melted marshmallows bring a little something different to this version of cream cheese frosting.

2 cups miniature marshmallows
8 ounces cream cheese, softened
8 tablespoons (1 stick) unsalted butter, softened
3 to 4 cups confectioners' sugar

1. Put the marshmallows in a microwave-safe bowl and microwave on High for 30 seconds. Stir, and continue to microwave in 10-second increments until the marshmallows are completely melted.

2. Beat the cream cheese and butter in a large bowl with an electric mixer until light and fluffy. Beat in the melted marshmallows. Gradually beat in enough confectioners' sugar to make a light, fluffy frosting. Spread on cooled cake or cupcakes. The frosting can be stored in the refrigerator. Bring to room temperature and beat again before using.

Quick Breads AND Breakfast Treats

Baked Donuts with Cream Cheese Frosting

If I have one weakness when it comes to food, it's donuts. It really takes every ounce of willpower I possess to stand in front of a box of donuts and not take one. So, in order to consume more donuts with a little bit less guilt, I started baking them. This version is the perfect way to start your day with a little bit of red velvet!

If you don't have a donut pan (which I suggest you buy—you won't be sorry!), you can bake these in muffin tins. **MAKES 12**

FOR THE DONUTS
1¾ cups all-purpose flour
¾ cup sugar
1½ teaspoons baking powder
¼ teaspoon baking soda
¼ teaspoon table salt
1 large egg
2 tablespoons unsalted butter, softened
1 tablespoon vegetable oil
1 teaspoon vanilla extract
½ cup buttermilk
2 teaspoons red liquid food coloring
1½ tablespoons natural unsweetened cocoa powder
1 teaspoon distilled white vinegar

FOR THE CREAM CHEESE FROSTING
2 ounces cream cheese, softened
1 tablespoon unsalted butter, softened
¼ teaspoon vanilla extract
A pinch of table salt
¾ cup confectioners' sugar
1 ounce white chocolate, melted and slightly cooled

1. Set a rack in the center position and preheat the oven to 350°F. Spray two 6-cavity donut pans with nonstick cooking spray.

2. To make the donuts: Whisk the flour, sugar, baking powder, baking soda, and salt in a bowl to combine. Add the egg, butter, vegetable oil, and vanilla and stir until combined.

RECIPE CONTINUES

3. Stir the buttermilk, food coloring, cocoa, and vinegar together in a measuring cup (make sure there are no lumps of cocoa). Add to the batter and mix just until combined.

4. Fill the cavities in the donut pan about one-half full with the batter. Bake until the donuts spring back when touched, 7 to 10 minutes. Remove from the pan and cool completely on a rack.

5. To make the frosting: Beat the cream cheese, butter, vanilla, and salt in a large bowl with an electric mixer until smooth. Gradually beat in the confectioners' sugar. Add the white chocolate and beat until light and fluffy.

6. Spread the frosting over the tops of the cooled donuts.

OPPOSITE:
Baked Donuts with Cream Cheese Frosting

Glazed Fried Donuts

There really is nothing like a fresh, hot, homemade donut. Although frying donuts may seem intimidating at first, once you try it, you'll see how rewarding (and delicious) it is. But don't blame me if you eat a dozen of them! MAKES 24 TO 30

FOR THE DONUTS
2 (¼-ounce) packages active dry yeast
¼ cup warm water
1½ cups lukewarm milk
½ cup sugar
1 teaspoon table salt
2 large eggs
⅓ cup vegetable shortening
5 cups all-purpose flour
1 tablespoon natural unsweetened cocoa powder
1 tablespoon red liquid food coloring
Vegetable oil, for deep-frying

FOR THE GLAZE
2 cups confectioners' sugar
2 tablespoons hot water
1 tablespoon milk
½ teaspoon vanilla extract

1. To make the donuts: Stir the yeast into the warm water and set aside until the mixture looks creamy, about 5 minutes.

2. Combine the milk, sugar, and salt in the bowl of a stand mixer fitted with the paddle attachment. Beat in the eggs, one at a time, scraping down the sides of the bowl after each addition. Beat in the shortening and 2 cups of the flour.

3. Combine the cocoa and the food coloring in a small bowl, stirring to make a smooth paste. Add to the dough and mix well.

4. Continue to add flour, ½ cup at a time, until the dough starts to pull away from the sides of the bowl. Remove the paddle attachment and use a dough hook to knead the dough until it is soft but not sticky, 5 to 8 minutes. Turn the dough out onto a lightly floured surface and form into a ball. Place in a large oiled bowl and turn to coat the dough with oil. Cover with plastic wrap and let rise until doubled in size, about 1½ hours.

5. Fill a Dutch oven or heavy-bottomed pot with oil to a depth of a few inches and heat to 350°F over medium heat. Cut the dough into quarters. Working with one quarter at a time,

RECIPE CONTINUES

roll out the dough on a lightly floured surface to a thickness of about ¼ inch. Use a 3-inch round cookie cutter to cut circles. Use a smaller round cutter to cut a hole in the center of each circle. Discard the scraps.

6. Line a baking sheet with paper towels. Carefully slide a few of the donuts into the hot oil. Fry until lightly browned, 30 to 45 seconds, then flip and cook the second side for about 30 seconds. Transfer to the prepared baking sheet.

7. To make the glaze: While the donuts are cooling, combine the confectioners' sugar, water, milk, and vanilla in a small bowl and stir until smooth. Dip the warm donuts in the glaze, turning to coat completely. Place the donuts on a rack until the glaze is set.

Red Velvet Crepes

I think crepes intimidate some people, but once you try them, you'll see just how easy they are to make. You can always fill these with fruit (they are great with strawberries), but I love this cream cheese filling. It really lends them that familiar red velvet flavor. **MAKES 20**

FOR THE CREPES
1⅓ cups milk
1 cup all-purpose flour
2 large eggs
3 tablespoons sugar
2 tablespoons vegetable oil
1½ tablespoons red liquid food coloring
1 tablespoon natural unsweetened cocoa powder
Confectioners' sugar, for topping

FOR THE CREAM CHEESE FILLING
8 ounces cream cheese, softened
¼ cup confectioners' sugar
1 tablespoon milk

1. To make the crepes: Combine the milk, flour, eggs, sugar, vegetable oil, food coloring, and cocoa powder in a blender. Blend until smooth. Let rest for 30 minutes.

2. Heat an 8-inch nonstick frying pan or crepe pan over medium-high heat. Add a small amount of butter to the pan to coat it. When the butter is melted, add about ¼ cup of batter to the pan, tilting and rotating the pan to coat the surface completely. Cook the crepe until the edges start to dry out, about 2 minutes. Loosen the edges with a spatula and turn the crepe. Cook the second side just until done, 30 seconds to 1 minute. Repeat with the remaining batter. Stack the crepes on a plate and cover with foil to keep warm.

3. To make the filling: Beat the cream cheese in a medium bowl until smooth. Beat in the confectioners' sugar and milk.

4. To assemble, spread a small amount of the cream cheese filling down the center of a crepe. Roll up the crepe and dust with confectioners' sugar. Repeat with the remaining crepes.

Crepe Cake

You can use 1 batch of Red Velvet Crepes to make this delicious dessert, but you can make the cake even more impressive by doubling the recipe and stacking the crepes twice as high.

Prepare the crepes as directed. For a cake made with 1 batch of crepes, beat 8 ounces cream cheese and 4 tablespoons (½ stick) softened unsalted butter in a mixing bowl with an electric mixer until smooth and fluffy.

Beat in 1 cup confectioners' sugar and ¼ teaspoon vanilla extract.

Place one crepe on a cake plate. With an offset spatula, cover the crepe with about 1 tablespoon of the cream cheese filling. Top with another crepe and more filling, and repeat until all crepes have been used. Refrigerate the cake until the filling is set, 1 to 2 hours. Dust with confectioners' sugar before serving.

OPPOSITE:
Red Velvet Crepes

Red Velvet Waffles

For some reason, waffles always remind me of vacation. Maybe it's because I associate them with hotels where you can make your own waffles for breakfast. So when I make them at home, it always feels like a special occasion. These waffles would be perfect for a holiday or celebration, or any time you want breakfast to feel a little noteworthy. They are amazing topped with Cream Cheese Drizzle (page 31), but I also love them with just a drizzle of maple syrup. **SERVES 6**

2 cups all-purpose flour
1 teaspoon baking soda
1 teaspoon baking powder
½ teaspoon table salt
4 tablespoons (½ stick) unsalted butter, melted
¼ cup packed brown sugar
3 large eggs, separated
2 cups buttermilk
1½ tablespoons natural unsweetened cocoa powder
1 tablespoon red liquid food coloring

1. Preheat the oven to 200°F and preheat a waffle iron. Whisk the flour, baking soda, baking powder, and salt in a large bowl to combine.

2. Combine the melted butter and brown sugar in a separate large bowl. Whisk in the egg yolks and buttermilk. Mix the cocoa powder and red food coloring in a small bowl to make a smooth paste, then whisk the paste into the butter mixture. Stir the wet ingredients into the dry ingredients just until moistened (the batter should be slightly lumpy).

3. Beat the egg whites in a medium bowl with an electric mixer until stiff peaks form. Stir one-quarter of the egg whites into the batter to lighten it. Then fold in the remaining egg whites gently but thoroughly.

4. Spray a waffle iron with nonstick cooking spray or brush with melted butter. Cook the waffles according to the manufacturer's instructions. As they're done, put them on a baking sheet and slide them into the oven to keep them warm while you cook the remaining waffles.

Light and Fluffy Pancakes

If it were up to my kids, we would eat pancakes for breakfast just about every day. Thank goodness, because we went through quite a few versions of these pancakes before I was happy with them! I'm a light-and-fluffy-pancake kind of girl, so folding in the whipped egg whites is a must in my book. If you like your pancakes more on the flat side, don't separate the eggs. MAKES 12

FOR THE PANCAKES

1½ cups all-purpose flour
3 tablespoons sugar
1 tablespoon baking powder
2 teaspoons natural unsweetened cocoa powder
¾ teaspoon table salt
1½ cups milk
2 large eggs, separated
3 tablespoons vegetable oil
2 tablespoons red liquid food coloring

FOR THE CREAM CHEESE DRIZZLE

4 ounces cream cheese, softened
¾ cup confectioners' sugar
½ teaspoon vanilla extract
A pinch of table salt
3 to 4 tablespoons milk

1. Preheat the oven to 200°F.

2. To make the pancakes: Whisk the flour, sugar, baking powder, cocoa, and salt in a large bowl to combine. Whisk the milk, egg yolks, oil, and red food coloring in a separate bowl. Stir the wet ingredients into the dry ingredients just until moistened (some lumps should remain).

3. Beat the egg whites in a medium bowl with an electric mixer until stiff peaks form. Stir one-third of the egg whites into the pancake batter to lighten it. Then fold in the remaining whites gently but thoroughly.

4. Heat a large griddle over medium heat. Spray with nonstick cooking spray or brush melted butter over the griddle. For each pancake, pour ⅓ cup of the batter onto the hot griddle. Cook until the surface starts to bubble, and the edges dry out, then flip and cook the second side. Put the pancakes onto a baking sheet and slide the sheet into the oven to keep warm while you cook the remaining batter.

5. To make the cream cheese drizzle: Beat the cream cheese, confectioners' sugar, vanilla, and salt in a bowl. Beat in enough milk to make a pourable mixture.

6. Serve the pancakes with the cream cheese drizzle.

French Toast with Caramel Syrup

Whenever I find myself with some bread that is a few days old, I turn to French toast. It's an easy breakfast the whole family loves, and I get to use up something that might go to waste otherwise. But this French toast is so good that it's worth making a loaf of Red Velvet Bread just for this recipe.

SERVES 6

FOR THE FRENCH TOAST

3 large eggs
¾ cup milk
1 teaspoon sugar
¼ teaspoon ground cinnamon
1 loaf Red Velvet Bread (page 87), cut into
    12 slices

FOR THE CARAMEL SYRUP

4 tablespoons (½ stick) unsalted butter
1 cup packed brown sugar
¼ cup water

1. Preheat a griddle over medium heat. Spray with nonstick cooking spray or brush with melted butter.

2. Beat the eggs lightly in a shallow bowl. Beat in the milk, sugar, and cinnamon. Dip each slice of bread into the egg mixture, coating both sides of the bread. Allow any excess egg mixture to drip off. Set the slices of bread on the griddle and cook, turning once, until golden brown on each side, 2 to 3 minutes per side.

3. To make the caramel syrup: Melt the butter in a small saucepan. Add the brown sugar and water and cook, stirring often, until the mixture comes to a boil. Boil until syrupy, about 2 minutes.

4. Serve the French toast with the caramel syrup.

Cream Cheese Muffins

Just when I thought I had seen it all, I spotted a package of red velvet muffins in the grocery store. Why had I never even thought of making them? I decided, though, that if I were going to do a red velvet muffin, there needed to be a cream cheese component to them as well—and a crumb topping. After all, they're muffins! MAKES 12

FOR THE MUFFINS
1¼ cups all-purpose flour
¾ cup sugar
2 teaspoons baking powder
½ teaspoon table salt
⅓ cup buttermilk
2 tablespoons natural unsweetened cocoa powder
1½ teaspoons red liquid food coloring
½ cup vegetable oil
1 large egg, slightly beaten
4 ounces cream cheese, softened

FOR THE CRUMB TOPPING
½ cup sugar
¼ cup all-purpose flour
2 tablespoons unsalted butter, cut into cubes

1. Preheat the oven to 375°F. Line a 12-cavity muffin tin with paper liners or spray with non-stick cooking spray.

2. To make the muffins: Whisk the flour, ½ cup of the sugar, the baking powder, and salt in a large bowl to combine. Whisk the buttermilk, cocoa, food coloring, oil, and egg in a separate bowl. Stir the wet ingredients into the dry just until moistened (some lumps should remain).

3. Beat the cream cheese and remaining ¼ cup sugar in a small bowl. Fold into the muffin batter, being careful to not overmix (some streaks of the cream cheese mixture should remain). Fill the muffin tins two-thirds full with the batter.

4. To make the crumb topping: Stir the sugar and flour in a bowl to combine. Add the butter and cut it in with two knives or a pastry blender until you have coarse crumbs. Sprinkle the crumb topping evenly over the muffins.

5. Bake until a toothpick inserted comes out clean, 17 to 20 minutes. Cool in the pan for 10 minutes, then remove to a rack to cool completely.

Breakfast Biscuits with Chocolate Gravy

I'm not a Southern girl, but sometimes I think I should have been. I am smitten by Southern food, and I am a huge fan of biscuits and gravy. Now, this is not your typical biscuits and gravy. We are sticking to Southern roots with the chocolate gravy, but red velvet biscuits are a new twist. Why these aren't served at every Southern restaurant is beyond me! **SERVES 6**

FOR THE BISCUITS

2¼ cups all-purpose flour, plus additional as needed

2 tablespoons sugar

3½ teaspoons baking powder

2 teaspoons natural unsweetened cocoa powder

1 teaspoon table salt

8 tablespoons (1 stick) unsalted butter, softened, plus 4 tablespoons (½ stick) unsalted butter, melted

1¼ cups buttermilk

1 tablespoon red liquid food coloring

FOR THE CHOCOLATE GRAVY

4 tablespoons (½ stick) unsalted butter

¼ cup all-purpose flour

⅔ cup sugar

⅓ cup natural unsweetened cocoa powder

2 cups milk

1. Set a rack in the center position and preheat the oven to 450°F. Spray a baking sheet with nonstick cooking spray.

2. To make the biscuits: Whisk the flour, sugar, baking powder, cocoa, and salt in a large bowl to combine. Using a pastry cutter, cut the 8 tablespoons of softened butter into the dry ingredients until it resembles coarse crumbs. Pour in the buttermilk and food coloring, and stir to combine.

3. Dump the biscuit dough out onto a floured work surface. Knead the dough 4 or 5 times, adding more flour if it's too sticky. Pat the dough into a rectangle about ¾ inch thick. Fold each side of the dough over to the center, as if you are folding a letter. Roll back out into a rectangle and repeat. Roll and repeat two more times.

RECIPE CONTINUES

4. Pat the dough into a 9 x 12-inch rectangle. Use a pizza cutter to cut the dough into 3 rows, then cut each row into 4 pieces, forming 12 biscuits. Transfer the biscuits to the baking sheet and bake until browned, 12 to 15 minutes. Remove from the oven and immediately brush with the 4 tablespoons of melted butter.

5. To make the chocolate gravy: Melt the butter in a medium skillet over medium heat. Whisk in the flour and cook, whisking, until the flour is completely incorporated, 1 to 2 minutes. Whisk in the sugar and cocoa, and then slowly whisk in the milk. Cook, whisking constantly, until thickened and bubbly.

6. Serve the biscuits topped with the chocolate gravy.

Cakes

AND

Cupcakes

Rocky Road Pie

What could be better than cake topped with a mountain of whipped cream, marshmallows, chocolate chips, and pecans? While this is technically not a pie at all, it is served in a pie dish. I've been eating a chocolate version of this cake ever since I can remember. **MAKES ONE 9-INCH CAKE**

FOR THE CAKE

1 cup plus 2 tablespoons all-purpose flour
1 tablespoon natural unsweetened cocoa powder
½ teaspoon table salt
¼ cup vegetable oil
¾ cup sugar
1 large egg
¼ cup buttermilk
2 tablespoons red liquid food coloring
½ teaspoon vanilla extract
½ teaspoon distilled white vinegar
½ teaspoon baking soda

FOR THE TOPPING

1¾ cups heavy cream
½ cup confectioners' sugar
2 tablespoons natural unsweetened cocoa powder
½ teaspoon vanilla extract
⅔ cup miniature marshmallows
⅔ cup chopped pecans
½ cup semisweet chocolate chips

1. To make the cake: Set a rack in the center position and preheat the oven to 350°F. Spray a 9-inch pie pan with nonstick cooking spray.

2. Whisk the flour, cocoa, and salt in a bowl to combine.

3. Beat the oil and sugar in a large bowl. Beat in the egg and then scrape down the sides of the bowl. Stir one-third of the dry ingredients into the sugar mixture, then stir in one-half of the buttermilk. Stir in the remaining dry ingredients and buttermilk in alternating additions. Stir in the red food coloring and vanilla.

4. Combine the vinegar and baking soda in a small bowl (it will bubble up). Fold into the cake batter. Spread the batter in the pie pan and bake until the cake springs back when lightly touched, 30 to 35 minutes. Let the cake cool completely on a rack.

5. To make the topping: Whip the heavy cream in a large bowl with an electric mixer until the cream starts to thicken, then gradually add the confectioners' sugar, cocoa, and vanilla. Continue until the cream forms stiff peaks.

6. Gently fold the marshmallows, pecans, and chocolate chips into the whipped cream. Pile the topping onto the cooled cake. Refrigerate until ready to serve.

Red Velvet Cheesecake

One of my all-time favorite desserts is cheesecake. With its bright red color, this cheesecake is definitely holiday-worthy. Top it with freshly whipped cream and chocolate curls to make it even more of a showstopper. **MAKES ONE 9-INCH CHEESECAKE**

20 whole chocolate graham crackers

12 tablespoons (1½ sticks) unsalted butter, cut into cubes

½ cup packed brown sugar

4 (8-ounce) packages cream cheese, softened

1½ cups granulated sugar

¾ cup milk

4 large eggs

1 cup sour cream

¼ cup all-purpose flour

3 tablespoons natural unsweetened cocoa powder

2 tablespoons red liquid food coloring

1. Set a rack in the center position and preheat the oven to 350°F. Wrap foil around the outside of a 9-inch springform pan.

2. Break up the graham crackers and put them in the bowl of a food processor, along with the butter and brown sugar. Process until the graham crackers are reduced to crumbs and the mixture starts to stick together. Press the crumbs into the bottom and halfway up the sides of the springform pan. Bake the crust for 10 minutes, then set it aside to cool while you prepare the cheesecake.

3. Beat the cream cheese, granulated sugar, and milk in a large bowl with an electric mixer until smooth. Beat in the eggs, one at a time, scraping down the sides of the bowl after each addition, being careful not to overbeat. (Overbeating the batter can add too much air to the cheesecake, causing it to rise and then fall, which will make cracks on the surface.) Mix in the sour cream, flour, cocoa, and red food coloring. Pour the batter into the springform pan.

4. Place the springform pan in a larger pan, and place both pans in the oven. Using a kettle or a large measuring cup, carefully pour hot water to a depth of about 1 inch into the larger pan.

5. Bake the cheesecake until the edges are set but the center is still a little bit wiggly, about 1 hour. Turn off the oven, but do not open the oven door. Leave the cheesecake in the oven for 5 to 6 hours. Remove from the oven and refrigerate until completely chilled.

6. To serve, run a knife around the edge of the pan, then carefully loosen the sides. Use a knife that has been dipped in hot water then dried with a paper towel to make clean cuts in the cheesecake.

Cheesecake Cake

The first time I saw a cheesecake cake, I knew I needed to make one immediately. What could be better than a layer of cheesecake sandwiched between two layers of red velvet cake? I sift cocoa powder over the top of the cake, but for even more drama, top the cake with chocolate curls.

You'll need to start this recipe the day before you want to serve it to give the cheesecake enough time to chill. **MAKES ONE 9-INCH CAKE**

FOR THE CHEESECAKE LAYER
20 ounces cream cheese, softened
¾ cup sugar
½ teaspoon finely grated lemon zest
¼ teaspoon table salt
2 large eggs
½ cup sour cream

FOR THE CAKE LAYERS
2¼ cups all-purpose flour
2 tablespoons natural unsweetened cocoa powder
1 teaspoon table salt
8 tablespoons (1 stick) unsalted butter, softened
1½ cups sugar
2 large eggs
1 cup buttermilk
4 tablespoons red liquid food coloring
1 teaspoon vanilla extract
1 teaspoon distilled white vinegar
1 teaspoon baking soda

FOR THE FROSTING
12 ounces cream cheese, softened
1½ cups (3 sticks) unsalted butter, softened
1½ teaspoons vanilla extract
3 cups confectioners' sugar
Natural unsweetened cocoa powder, for dusting

1. To make the cheesecake layer: Set a rack in the center position and preheat the oven to 325°F. Line the bottom of a 9-inch springform pan with parchment paper. Wrap the outside of the pan in foil.

2. Beat the cream cheese in a large bowl with an electric mixer until fluffy. Gradually beat in the sugar. Add the lemon zest and salt and beat to combine. Beat in the eggs, one at a time, scraping down the sides of the bowl after each addition, being careful to not overbeat. Beat in the sour cream.

RECIPE CONTINUES

3. Pour the batter into the springform pan. Place the springform pan in a larger pan and place both pans in the oven. Using a kettle or a large measuring cup, carefully pour hot water to a depth of about 1 inch into the larger pan. Bake just until the cheesecake is set, about 45 minutes. Allow the cheesecake to cool on a rack for at least 1 hour, then chill it in the refrigerator overnight. Remove the cheesecake from the pan, wrap it in plastic wrap, and freeze for 4 to 5 hours or overnight. (The cheesecake can be stored frozen, well wrapped, for up to 2 months.)

4. To make the cake layers: Set a rack in the center position and preheat the oven to 350°F. Line the bottoms of two 9-inch cake pans with parchment paper. Spray the pans and the parchment paper with nonstick cooking spray.

5. Whisk the flour, cocoa, and salt in a bowl to combine. Beat the butter and sugar in a large bowl with an electric mixer on medium speed until fluffy, about 5 minutes. Beat in the eggs, one at a time, scraping down the sides of the bowl after each addition. Add the dry ingredients and the buttermilk to the butter mixture in two or three alternating additions, mixing until combined. Mix in the red food coloring and vanilla.

6. Combine the vinegar and baking soda in a small bowl (it will bubble up). Fold into the cake batter. Divide the batter evenly between the baking pans. Bake until the cakes spring back when lightly touched, 30 to 35 minutes. Let the cakes cool in the pans for 10 minutes, then turn out onto a rack to cool completely.

7. To make the frosting: Beat the cream cheese, butter, and vanilla in a large bowl with an electric mixer until light and fluffy. Gradually beat in the confectioners' sugar, then continue to beat until the frosting is light and fluffy, 5 to 7 minutes.

8. To assemble the cake: If necessary, slice off the tops of the cakes to level the layers. Place one cake layer on a cake stand or serving platter. Remove the cheesecake from the freezer and unwrap. Place on top of the cake layer. If necessary, trim the sides of the cheesecake so it is even with the cake layer. Place the second cake layer on top of the cheesecake. Coat the entire cake with a thin layer of the frosting, forming a crumb coat. Refrigerate the cake for 30 minutes. Frost the cake with the remaining frosting. Dust the top of the cake with cocoa powder. Refrigerate until ready to serve.

Cake Roll

I have made many, many pumpkin cake rolls during the fall. But I've decided that cake rolls deserve to be enjoyed year round! My mom makes a great chocolate cake roll, but I'm pretty sure this red velvet version rivals hers. **MAKES ONE 9-INCH CAKE ROLL**

FOR THE CAKE

3 large eggs
1 cup sugar
⅓ cup hot water
1 teaspoon vanilla extract
1½ tablespoons red liquid food coloring
2 teaspoons natural unsweetened cocoa powder
1 cup all-purpose flour
1 teaspoon baking powder
¼ teaspoon table salt
Confectioners' sugar for dusting

FOR THE FILLING

3 tablespoons unsalted butter, softened
12 ounces cream cheese, softened
1⅓ cups confectioners' sugar
½ teaspoon vanilla extract

1. To make the cake: Set a rack in the center position and preheat the oven to 375°F. Line a 9 x 13-inch jelly roll pan with parchment paper, then butter the parchment paper.

2. Beat the eggs in a mixing bowl with an electric mixer until very light, about 5 minutes. Gradually beat in the sugar. Add the water and the vanilla and mix to combine.

3. Combine the food coloring and cocoa in a small bowl to make a smooth paste. Add to the egg mixture and beat to combine.

4. Whisk the flour, baking powder, and salt in a bowl to combine. Fold the dry ingredients into the egg mixture.

5. Pour the batter into the pan and bake just until set in the center, about 15 minutes. Turn the cake out onto a tea towel that has been generously dusted with confectioners' sugar. Peel off the parchment paper and roll the cake up with the towel. Cool completely.

6. To make the filling: Beat the butter and cream cheese in a mixing bowl with an electric mixer until light and fluffy. Add the confectioners' sugar and beat until smooth. Beat in the vanilla.

RECIPE CONTINUES

7. Carefully unroll the cake. Spread the filling over the surface of the cake, leaving a ½-inch border on all sides. Carefully roll the cake back up without the towel, and place the cake, seam side down, on a serving dish. Dust with confectioners' sugar and cut into slices to serve.

CAKE ROLL, *variation*

Mug Cake for One

Don't tell me I'm the only one who occasionally gets a cake craving that needs to be satisfied *right now*. Since I'm such a red velvet fan, I wanted a way to get that red velvet fix without leaving the house or having to make a whole cake, so I came up with this quick mug version for one.

Combine 2 tablespoons all-purpose flour, 2 tablespoons buttermilk, 3 tablespoons sugar, 1 teaspoon natural unsweetened cocoa powder, ½ teaspoon red liquid food coloring, ¼ teaspoon baking powder, ¼ teaspoon vanilla extract, and ⅛ teaspoon table salt into a large mug, stirring just until combined. Microwave on High until the cake springs back when touched in the center, 60 to 90 seconds.

Serve topped with confectioners' sugar or ice cream, if desired.

OPPOSITE: Cake Roll

Icebox Cake

There are quite a few types of icebox cake, but this is my favorite. You make red velvet graham crackers, layer them with whipped cream, and then refrigerate until the graham crackers become fork-tender. My dad has declared this his favorite red velvet dessert. **MAKES ONE 8-INCH CAKE**

FOR THE GRAHAM CRACKERS

2 tablespoons plus 2 teaspoons honey

2½ tablespoons buttermilk

1½ teaspoons red liquid food coloring

1 teaspoon vanilla extract

1¼ cups all-purpose flour

½ cup packed brown sugar

1 tablespoon natural unsweetened cocoa powder

½ teaspoon baking soda

¼ teaspoon table salt

3½ tablespoons unsalted butter, cut into small pieces

FOR THE FILLING

3 cups heavy cream

⅓ cup confectioners' sugar

1 teaspoon vanilla extract

1 tablespoon miniature chocolate chips

FOR THE FROSTING

½ cup heavy cream

3 tablespoons confectioners' sugar

FOR THE CHOCOLATE DRIZZLE

3 heaping tablespoons semisweet chocolate chips

1 tablespoon heavy cream

1. To make the graham crackers: Combine the honey, buttermilk, food coloring, and vanilla in a small bowl. Place the flour, brown sugar, cocoa, baking soda, and salt in the bowl of a food processor. Pulse to combine. Add the butter and pulse until rough crumbs form. Add the honey mixture and process just until the dough forms a ball. Wrap the dough in plastic wrap and chill for at least 2 hours.

2. Flour a work surface and roll the dough into an 8 x 16-inch rectangle. Use a pizza cutter to cut the dough into four 4 x 8-inch rectangles. Transfer to a parchment paper–lined baking sheet. Refrigerate for at least 1 hour.

3. Position oven racks in the upper and lower thirds of the oven and preheat the oven to 350°F. Poke the crackers all over with a toothpick, then bake until they start to brown on the edges, 15 to 25 minutes, rotating the baking sheets halfway through the cooking time. Cool completely.

4. To make the filling: Whip the heavy cream in a mixing bowl with an electric mixer until soft peaks form. Gradually add the confectioners' sugar and vanilla and beat until stiff peaks form.

5. Line a 4 x 8-inch loaf pan with plastic wrap, making sure the ends extend well over the rim of the pan. Spread a thin layer of the filling over the bottom of the pan. Set a graham cracker on top of the filling, trimming if necessary to make it fit in the pan. Spread one-third of the remaining filling over the graham cracker, then sprinkle 1 teaspoon of the chocolate chips over the filling. Repeat the layers, ending with a graham cracker layer. Fold the overhanging plastic wrap over the cake and refrigerate for at least 4 hours.

6. To make the frosting: Whip the cream in a mixing bowl with an electric mixer until soft peaks form. Gradually add the confectioners' sugar and beat until stiff peaks form.

7. Remove the cake from the refrigerator. Pull back the plastic wrap, then invert the pan onto a serving platter. Carefully remove the plastic wrap. Frost the cake with the frosting.

8. To make the chocolate drizzle: Combine the chocolate chips and cream in a small bowl and microwave on High in 10-second increments until the chips are melted. Stir until smooth. Drizzle over the top of the cake and serve.

Molten Lava Cakes

I used to think of molten lava cakes as something you could enjoy only at a restaurant. Then I discovered how easy this fancy dessert is to make at home. The cakes need to be baked right before serving, but they can be made ahead up to that point and refrigerated. If you aren't a fan of the molten center, just cook the cake a few minutes more, until it is cooked through the center. **MAKES 4**

8 tablespoons (1 stick) unsalted butter
4 ounces white chocolate
1 cup confectioners' sugar
2 large eggs
2 large egg yolks
1 tablespoon red liquid food coloring
2 teaspoons natural unsweetened cocoa powder
6 tablespoons all-purpose flour
Confectioners' sugar, for dusting
Raspberries or sliced strawberries, for serving

1. Set a rack in the center position and preheat the oven to 450°F. Spray four 6-ounce ramekins generously with nonstick cooking spray.

2. Melt the butter and white chocolate in the top of a double boiler, stirring until smooth. When completely melted, stir in the confectioners' sugar.

3. Lightly whisk the eggs and egg yolks in a large bowl. Stir in the red food coloring and melted chocolate mixture.

4. Whisk the cocoa and flour in a small bowl to combine. Add to the batter and stir just until combined.

5. Divide the batter evenly among the ramekins. Place the ramekins on a baking sheet and bake until the sides of the cakes are set but the centers are still soft, 14 to 15 minutes. Let the cakes rest for 2 minutes, then invert them onto dessert plates.

6. Serve the cakes immediately, dusted with confectioners' sugar and with berries on the side.

Bundt Cake with Cream Cheese Icing

If I need a dessert for a potluck, I often bring a Bundt cake. They are easy to make ahead of time, and they always look impressive. Make sure your pan is completely greased for this one so the cake will come out of the pan easily. But even if you have a few less-than-perfect spots, you'll most likely be able to disguise them with the sweet, thick icing. **MAKES ONE 10-INCH CAKE**

FOR THE CAKE

3 cups all-purpose flour
2 tablespoons natural unsweetened cocoa powder
1 teaspoon baking powder
½ teaspoon baking soda
¼ teaspoon table salt
2 tablespoons red liquid food coloring
1 cup buttermilk
1 cup (2 sticks) unsalted butter, softened
2⅓ cups sugar
3 large eggs
1 teaspoon vanilla extract

FOR THE ICING

4 ounces cream cheese, softened
½ cup confectioners' sugar
1 teaspoon vanilla extract
2 to 3 tablespoons milk

1. To make the cake: Set a rack in the center position and preheat the oven to 350°F. Butter and flour a 12-cup Bundt pan generously.

2. Whisk the flour, cocoa, baking powder, baking soda, and salt in a bowl to combine. Stir the food coloring into the buttermilk.

3. Beat the butter and sugar in a large bowl with an electric mixer until light and fluffy. Beat in the eggs, one at a time, scraping down the sides of the bowl after each addition. Add the dry ingredients and the buttermilk to the creamed butter and sugar in alternating additions, starting and finishing with the dry ingredients and mixing just until combined; do not overmix. Pour the batter into the Bundt pan. Smooth the top.

4. Bake until a tester inserted in the cake comes out clean, 50 to 55 minutes. Cool for 10 minutes, then invert the cake onto a serving plate. Let the cake cool completely before removing the pan.

5. To make the icing: Beat the cream cheese and confectioners' sugar in a mixing bowl with an electric mixer until smooth. Beat in the vanilla, then add in the milk, 1 tablespoon at a time, until the mixture reaches a pourable consistency. Slowly pour the icing over the cooled cake.

Cheesecake Surprise Cupcakes

This is another recipe inspired by my childhood. Every Sunday, we would go over to my grandparents' house, and my mom would bring dessert. My favorite? Chocolate cheesecake cupcakes, a chocolate cupcake with a cream cheese center. My version takes a red velvet cupcake, gives it a cheesecake center, and then takes it over the top with a luscious chocolate icing.

I loved eating my mom's cupcakes straight out of the refrigerator, and these are just as good when they're chilled. MAKES 30

FOR THE CUPCAKES
2¼ cups all-purpose flour
1 teaspoon table salt
1½ cups sugar
1 cup vegetable oil
2 large eggs
3 tablespoons red liquid food coloring
1 tablespoon natural unsweetened cocoa powder
1 cup buttermilk
1½ teaspoons vanilla extract
1 teaspoon baking soda
1 teaspoon distilled white vinegar

FOR THE FILLING
8 ounces cream cheese, softened
½ cup confectioners' sugar
1 large egg
A pinch of table salt
¾ cup miniature chocolate chips

FOR THE ICING
4 ounces semisweet chocolate chips

5⅓ tablespoons (⅓ cup) unsalted butter, cut into pieces
2 tablespoons light corn syrup
½ teaspoon vanilla extract

1. To make the cupcakes: Position oven racks in the upper and lower thirds of the oven and preheat the oven to 350°F. Line two 12-cavity muffin tins with paper liners and one 12-cavity muffin tin with 6 paper liners.

2. Whisk the flour and salt in a bowl to combine. Beat the sugar and oil in a mixing bowl with an electric mixer until thoroughly combined. Beat in the eggs one at a time, beating for 30 seconds and scraping down the sides of the bowl after each addition. Mix the food coloring and cocoa in a small bowl and add to the sugar mixture; mix well. Add the dry ingredients and the buttermilk to the sugar mixture in two or three alternating additions, mixing until combined. Stir in the vanilla.

3. Combine the baking soda and vinegar in a small bowl (it will bubble up) and fold it into the batter. Spoon the batter into the lined muffin tins. Set aside.

4. To make the filling: Beat the cream cheese and confectioners' sugar in a mixing bowl with an electric mixer until smooth. Beat in the egg and salt. Stir in the chocolate chips. Drop 1 heaping tablespoonful of the filling on top of each cupcake.

5. Bake until the cupcakes feel springy to the touch, 15 to 20 minutes. Cool completely on racks.

6. To make the icing: Combine the chocolate chips, butter, and corn syrup in a small bowl. Microwave on High for 1 minute, then stir until the chocolate has completely melted and the icing is smooth. Stir in the vanilla. Dip the top of each cooled cupcake into the chocolate icing. Return the cupcakes to the racks to allow the icing to set.

Red Velvet Snowballs

These cream-filled cupcakes, covered in marshmallow and coconut, are irresistible. I might even be so bold as to claim that this homemade version is even better than store-bought. I do have to warn you that these are very messy to assemble, but they are definitely worth the sticky hands. MAKES 12

FOR THE CUPCAKES

1 cup plus 2 tablespoons all-purpose flour
½ teaspoon table salt
1½ teaspoons natural unsweetened cocoa powder
¾ cup sugar
½ cup vegetable oil
1 large egg
3 teaspoons red liquid food coloring
½ cup buttermilk
¾ teaspoon vanilla extract
½ teaspoon distilled white vinegar
½ teaspoon baking soda

FOR THE MARSHMALLOW FILLING

1 cup marshmallow crème
4 tablespoons (½ stick) unsalted butter, softened
½ cup confectioners' sugar

FOR THE MARSHMALLOW COATING

3 cups shredded sweetened coconut
¾ teaspoon red liquid food coloring
4 cups confectioners' sugar
1 (7-ounce) container marshmallow crème
4 tablespoons (½ stick) unsalted butter, softened
1 teaspoon vanilla extract
2 to 3 tablespoons milk

1. To make the cupcakes: Set a rack in the center position and preheat the oven to 350°F. Line a 12-cavity muffin tin with paper liners.

2. Whisk the flour, salt, and cocoa in a bowl to combine.

3. Beat the sugar and oil in a large bowl with an electric mixer until smooth. Add the egg and mix well. Mix in the red food coloring. Add the dry ingredients and the buttermilk to the sugar mixture in two or three alternating additions, mixing until combined. Stir in the vanilla.

4. Combine the vinegar and baking soda in a small bowl (it will bubble up). Fold into the batter. Fill the cupcake liners about two-thirds full with batter. Bake until a tester inserted in the center of a cupcake comes out clean, about 18 minutes. Cool for 5 minutes, then remove to a rack to cool completely.

5. To make the marshmallow filling: Beat the marshmallow crème, butter, and confectioners' sugar in a medium bowl with an electric mixer until smooth.

6. Remove the liners from the cooled cupcakes. Use a paring knife to cut a cone-shaped piece out of the center of each cupcake. Slice off the pointed ends of the cone-shaped pieces. If desired, carefully use a spoon to remove a bit more cake from the center of each cupcake, to make more room for filling. Fill each cupcake with a dollop of the filling, and place the trimmed cones of cupcake on top of the filling to enclose it.

7. To make the marshmallow coating: Coarsely chop the coconut. Place it in a bowl or a large zip-top plastic bag and add the food coloring. Stir or shake until all of the coconut has been dyed with the food coloring. Put the colored coconut in a shallow bowl.

8. Beat the confectioners' sugar, marshmallow crème, butter, vanilla, and 2 tablespoons of the milk in a large bowl with an electric mixer until fluffy. Beat in the remaining 1 tablespoon milk if the frosting is too stiff. Cover the cupcakes completely (the bottoms and sides as well as the tops) with the frosting, then roll them in the coconut. Place on waxed paper and let sit for 1 hour, to allow the frosting to set. These are best served the day they are made.

Cookies

Cookie Mix in a Jar

"Welcome to the neighborhood!" "Thank you." Or even "Just because." There are lots of reasons to have a fun gift on hand for when the moment strikes. As someone who loves food, I'm always on the lookout for foodie gifts. I love these "cookies in a jar" because the mix doesn't have to be used right away. And it doesn't hurt that the cookies are super tasty! Attach a bottle of red food coloring to the jar to make sure the recipient will have everything needed to make the cookies.

MIX MAKES ABOUT 40 COOKIES

½ cup sugar
½ cup semisweet chocolate chips
½ cup packed brown sugar
½ cup milk chocolate chips
¾ teaspoon baking soda
½ teaspoon baking powder
¼ teaspoon table salt
2 cups all-purpose flour

2 tablespoons natural unsweetened cocoa powder
½ cup white chocolate chips

1. Layer the ingredients in the order listed in a 1-quart wide-mouthed jar, packing down each addition.

2. Attach a tag with the following instructions:

> TO MAKE COOKIES: Preheat the oven to 350° F. Beat 8 tablespoons (1 stick) softened, unsalted butter in a large bowl with an electric mixer until fluffy. Beat in 1 large egg, 2 teaspoons vanilla extract, and 2 tablespoons red liquid food coloring. Add the contents of the jar, and stir until the dough comes together. Drop tablespoon-size balls of dough 2 inches apart onto ungreased baking sheets. Bake until the edges of the cookies are set, 10 to 12 minutes. Makes about 40 cookies.

Gooey Butter Cookies

When my cookie craving hits, I tend to want something gooey and soft rather than crisp. Well, cookies don't get much softer or gooier than these. With cream cheese as one of the main ingredients, these cookies are guaranteed to be soft and delicious. MAKES 36

2¼ cups all-purpose flour
2 cups granulated sugar
2 tablespoons natural unsweetened cocoa powder
2 teaspoons baking powder
¼ teaspoon table salt
8 ounces cream cheese, softened
4 tablespoons (½ stick) unsalted butter, softened
1 large egg
1 tablespoon red liquid food coloring
½ cup confectioners' sugar

1. Whisk the flour, granulated sugar, cocoa, baking powder, and salt in a bowl to combine.

2. Beat the cream cheese and butter in a large bowl with an electric mixer until smooth. Beat in the egg and food coloring.

3. Add the dry ingredients to the creamed mixture and mix until the dough comes together. Cover with plastic wrap and chill the dough for 2 hours.

4. When ready to bake, preheat the oven to 350°F. Line two baking sheets with parchment paper. Place the confectioners' sugar in a shallow bowl.

5. Roll the dough into balls (about 1 tablespoon each). Roll the dough balls in the confectioners' sugar, then place on the baking sheets at least 3 inches apart. Bake until the edges of the cookies are set, 10 to 12 minutes. Transfer the cookies to racks to cool completely. Store the cookies in an airtight container for up to 3 days.

Cookies with White Chocolate Chips

Super soft and full of white chocolate chips, these cookies are great for a midmorning pick-me-up or an after-school treat. Everyone needs a basic red velvet cookie recipe, and this one fits the bill.

MAKES 30

2¼ cups all-purpose flour
2 tablespoons natural unsweetened cocoa powder
1 teaspoon baking powder
¼ teaspoon table salt
1 cup (2 sticks) unsalted butter, softened
1 cup granulated sugar
½ cup packed brown sugar
2 large eggs
1½ tablespoons red liquid food coloring
1 teaspoon distilled white vinegar
1 teaspoon vanilla extract
1½ cups white chocolate chips

1. Whisk the flour, cocoa, baking powder, and salt in a bowl to combine.

2. Beat the butter with the granulated and brown sugars in a mixing bowl with an electric mixer until light and fluffy. Beat in the eggs, one at a time, scraping down the sides of the bowl after each addition. Beat in the food coloring, vinegar, and vanilla. Add the dry ingredients and mix until combined. Stir in the white chocolate chips. Cover with plastic wrap and refrigerate the dough for 1 hour.

3. When ready to bake, preheat the oven to 350°F. Line two baking sheets with parchment paper.

4. Form the dough into balls (about 2 tablespoons each). Place the dough balls at least 3 inches apart on the baking sheets. Bake until the cookies are set around the edges, 10 to 12 minutes. Let the cookies sit on the baking sheets for 2 minutes before transferring to racks to cool completely. Store the cookies in an airtight container for up to 3 days.

Whoopie Pies

When I was dating my husband, he claimed that the best whoopie pies ever were sold at a gas station in a town about an hour from where we lived. One day, we decided that I needed to experience these treats. We made the drive, only to find out that they didn't have any fresh whoopie pies that day. To this day, I still haven't tried one of those pies, but I'm pretty sure my husband now considers these whoopie pies his favorite.

If you don't have a pastry bag, you can substitute a zip-top plastic bag. Just snip off a corner of the bag after you've filled it. MAKES 18

FOR THE COOKIES

2 cups all-purpose flour
½ tablespoon natural unsweetened cocoa powder
1 teaspoon baking powder
1 teaspoon baking soda
½ teaspoon table salt
2 tablespoons red liquid food coloring
1 teaspoon vanilla extract
1 cup buttermilk
½ cup vegetable shortening
1 cup packed brown sugar
1 large egg

FOR THE FILLING

1 cup (2 sticks) unsalted butter, softened
1½ cups confectioners' sugar
1 (7-ounce) container marshmallow crème
1½ teaspoons vanilla extract

1. Preheat the oven to 350°F. Line two baking sheets with parchment paper.

2. Whisk the flour, cocoa, baking powder, baking soda, and salt in a bowl to combine. Stir the food coloring and vanilla into the buttermilk.

3. Beat the shortening and brown sugar in a mixing bowl with an electric mixer until fluffy. Beat in the egg. Add the dry ingredients and the buttermilk mixture to the shortening mixture in two or three alternating additions, mixing until combined.

4. Transfer the dough into a pastry bag. Pipe 36 circles of dough, about 2 inches in diameter, onto the baking sheets, keeping them about 2 inches apart. Smooth down any points of dough with a wet finger. Bake until the center springs back when touched, about 12 minutes. Cool completely on the baking sheets.

5. To make the filling: Beat the butter in a mixing bowl with an electric mixer until light and fluffy. Add the confectioners' sugar and beat to combine. Beat in the marshmallow crème and vanilla extract until smooth. Transfer the filling to a pastry bag. Pipe about 1 tablespoon of filling on the flat side of one cookie. Top with another cookie, flat side down. Repeat with the remaining cookies and filling. Store in an airtight container for up to 3 days.

Red Velvet "Oreos"

My grandma had a cookie jar (shaped like a dog) that always sat on her counter. She wasn't much of a baker, but there were always Double Stuf Oreos in that dog. It was a treat to get an Oreo or two (or three!) when we went to my grandparents' house on Sunday nights. I can imagine how happy my kids would be if I kept a jar filled with these cookies on my counter at all times. **MAKES 24**

FOR THE COOKIES
1½ cups all-purpose flour
2 tablespoons natural unsweetened cocoa powder
1 teaspoon baking soda
¼ teaspoon baking powder
¼ teaspoon table salt
1 cup sugar
8 tablespoons (1 stick) unsalted butter, softened
1 large egg
1 tablespoon red liquid food coloring

FOR THE FILLING
2 cups confectioners' sugar
½ cup vegetable shortening
8 tablespoons (1 stick) unsalted butter, softened

1 tablespoon hot water
½ teaspoon vanilla extract

1. To make the cookies: Position oven racks in the upper and lower thirds of the oven and preheat the oven to 375°F. Line two baking sheets with parchment paper.

2. Whisk the flour, cocoa, baking soda, baking powder, and salt in a bowl to combine. Beat the sugar and butter in a mixing bowl with an electric mixer until light and fluffy. Beat in the egg and food coloring. Add the dry ingredients and stir until the dough comes together.

RED VELVET "OREOS," *variation*

Ice Cream Sandwiches

Turn these cookies into ice cream sandwiches! Instead of the cream filling, fill the cookies with softened vanilla or cheesecake ice cream. Better yet, fill them with Cheesecake and Red Velvet Cake Ice Cream (page 97)! Wrap the sandwiches in plastic and freeze until firm.

3. Form the dough into balls (about 1 table-spoon each) and place the dough balls at least 3 inches apart on the baking sheets. Flatten the balls slightly with the bottom of a drinking glass. Bake until the edges start setting, 7 to 8 minutes. Cool for 5 minutes on the baking sheets, then transfer to racks to cool completely.

4. To make the filling: Beat the confectioners' sugar, shortening, butter, water, and vanilla in a mixing bowl with an electric mixer until light and fluffy.

5. Place the filling in a pastry bag fitted with a ½-inch round tip. Turn half the cookies over and pipe about 1 teaspoon of the filling onto the flat side of each cookie. Place another cookie on top of the filling, flat side down. Lightly press the cookies together to spread out the filling. Store in an airtight container for up to 3 days.

Cream Cheese Thumbprints

Could there be a better filling for red velvet thumbprint cookies than cream cheese? Bake these cookies until they start to set, then fill the indentations with a cream cheese mixture. Back into the oven they go until they are baked through. The sugar coating gives them a sparkle and crunch that's irresistible. MAKES 36

FOR THE COOKIES

1 cup (2 sticks) unsalted butter, softened
½ cup packed brown sugar
2 large eggs, separated
1 teaspoon vanilla extract
2 cups all-purpose flour
4 teaspoons red liquid food coloring
2 teaspoons natural unsweetened cocoa powder
½ cup granulated sugar

FOR THE FILLING

4 ounces cream cheese, softened
¼ cup sugar
⅛ teaspoon table salt
¼ teaspoon vanilla extract

1. To make the cookies: Preheat the oven to 300°F.

2. Beat the butter, brown sugar, and 1 egg yolk (reserve the other yolk for the filling) in a large bowl with an electric mixer until fluffy. Beat in the vanilla. Add the flour, food coloring, and cocoa and mix until a soft dough forms. Roll the dough into 36 balls.

3. Place the egg whites in a shallow bowl and beat them lightly with a fork. Place the granulated sugar in a separate shallow bowl. Roll each dough ball in the egg whites and then in the sugar. Place the balls 2 inches apart on ungreased baking sheets. Make an indentation in the top of each cookie with your thumb.

4. To make the filling: Beat the cream cheese, sugar, the reserved egg yolk, salt, and vanilla in a bowl with an electric mixer until smooth.

5. Bake the cookies for 10 minutes. Remove them from the oven and use the handle of a wooden spoon to deepen the indentations in the cookies (be careful not to break them). Fill each cookie with about 1 teaspoon of the filling, then return the cookies to the oven and bake until the cookies and fillings are set, about 12 minutes more. Cool for 2 minutes on the baking sheets, then transfer to a rack to cool completely. Store the cookies in the refrigerator. Allow the cookies to come to room temperature before serving.

Red Velvet Biscotti

These slightly sweet, crunchy cookies, dipped in white chocolate, are the perfect snack, in my opinion.
MAKES 36

1 tablespoon natural unsweetened cocoa powder
1 tablespoon red liquid food coloring
3¼ cups all-purpose flour
1 tablespoon baking powder
½ teaspoon table salt
1 cup sugar
½ cup vegetable oil
3 large eggs
1 teaspoon vanilla extract
8 ounces white chocolate, chopped

1. Position oven racks in the upper and lower thirds of the oven and preheat the oven to 375°F. Line two baking sheets with parchment paper.

2. Stir the cocoa and food coloring together in a small bowl to make a smooth paste. Whisk the flour, baking powder, and salt in a bowl to combine.

3. Beat the sugar, oil, eggs, and vanilla in a large bowl with an electric mixer. Add the cocoa mixture and mix well. Add the dry ingredients and stir until a soft dough forms.

4. Divide the dough in half. Form each piece of dough into a log on a baking sheet. Flatten the dough to form a rectangle about 4 inches wide, 15 inches long, and ½ inch thick.

5. Bake until the rectangles are just set, 25 to 30 minutes. Remove from the oven. (Leave the oven on.) When the rectangles are cool enough to handle, cut them into 1-inch-thick slices. Arrange the slices on their sides, cut side up, on the baking sheets and bake until they start to feel dry, 6 to 10 minutes more. Cool completely.

6. Melt the white chocolate in a heatproof bowl set over a pot of simmering water. Lay a sheet of waxed paper on a countertop or work surface. Dip half of each biscotti into the chocolate, allowing any excess to drip off. Place the biscotti on the waxed paper. Let sit until the chocolate has set completely. Store in an airtight container. These cookies will last several weeks.

Brownies AND Bars

Brownie Cups

The centers of these miniature red velvet brownies fall after baking, turning them into little cups that cry out for a delicious cream cheese filling. They're the perfect treat for both brownie lovers and frosting lovers! If you don't want to make the mini version, bake the batter in an 8-inch square baking dish and frost the cooled brownies with the filling.

You'll need two or three mini muffin tins, depending on how many cavities your pans have.

MAKES 36

FOR THE BROWNIES
1 cup all-purpose flour
1½ teaspoons baking powder
½ teaspoon table salt
1 teaspoon natural unsweetened cocoa powder
5⅓ tablespoons (⅓ cup) unsalted butter, melted
1 cup packed brown sugar
1 large egg
2 teaspoons red liquid food coloring
1 teaspoon vanilla extract

FOR THE FILLING
6 ounces cream cheese, softened
6 tablespoons (¾ stick) unsalted butter, softened
1½ cups confectioners' sugar

1. To make the brownies: Preheat the oven to 350°F. Spray mini muffin tins with nonstick cooking spray.

2. Whisk the flour, baking powder, salt, and cocoa in a bowl to combine.

3. Mix the melted butter and brown sugar in a large bowl. Stir in the egg, food coloring, and vanilla. Stir in the dry ingredients. Place about 1 tablespoon of batter into each muffin cavity. Bake until the brownies are set, 10 to 12 minutes. The brownies should naturally fall in the centers after baking, but if they don't, gently press down the centers with the handle of a wooden spoon. Cool completely in the tins.

4. To make the filling: Beat the cream cheese and butter until smooth. Gradually add the confectioners' sugar and beat until smooth.

5. Place the filling in a pastry bag fitted with a star tip. Remove the brownies from the tins and pipe the filling into the cups. Store the brownies in an airtight container in the refrigerator.

RECIPE CONTINUES

Cream Cheese Swirl Brownies

Preheat the oven to 350°F. Prepare the Brownie Cups batter. Reserve about ½ cup of the batter. Spread the remaining batter in the bottom of an 8-inch square baking dish sprayed with nonstick cooking spray.

Beat 8 ounces softened cream cheese, ¼ cup sugar, 1 large egg, and ½ teaspoon vanilla extract in a mixing bowl with an electric mixer until fluffy. Drop dollops of the cream cheese mixture over the brownie batter. Drop dollops of the reserved brownie batter over the cream cheese mixture. Gently swirl the batters with a butter knife, going lengthwise and cross-wise. Bake until a tester inserted in the center comes out clean, about 30 minutes. Let cool completely in the pan, then cut into squares.

OPPOSITE: Brownie Cups

Marshmallow Rockslide Brownies

Imagine red velvet brownies topped with marshmallows and a rich chocolate frosting, then finished with more brownie chunks on top. These are definitely indulgent! MAKES 20

FOR THE BROWNIES

3 cups all-purpose flour
1 tablespoon natural unsweetened cocoa powder
1½ teaspoons baking powder
1 teaspoon table salt
½ teaspoon baking soda
1 cup (2 sticks) unsalted butter, melted
3 cups packed brown sugar
3 large eggs
2 tablespoons red liquid food coloring
2 teaspoons vanilla extract

FOR THE TOPPING

4 cups miniature marshmallows
4 tablespoons (½ stick) unsalted butter
3 tablespoons natural unsweetened cocoa powder
3 tablespoons milk
2 cups confectioners' sugar
½ teaspoon vanilla extract

1. To make the brownies: Preheat the oven to 350°F. Spray an 8-inch square baking dish and a 9 x 13-inch baking dish with nonstick cooking spray.

2. Whisk the flour, cocoa, baking powder, salt, and baking soda in a bowl to combine.

3. Stir the melted butter and brown sugar in a large bowl to combine. Stir in the eggs. Stir in the red food coloring and vanilla. Stir in the dry ingredients. Pour 1 cup of the batter into the 8-inch square baking dish and the remaining batter into the 9 x 13-inch baking dish.

4. Bake until a tester inserted in the center of the brownies comes out clean, 20 to 23 minutes for the smaller pan and 40 to 45 minutes for the larger pan. Cool completely on racks. Remove the brownies from the smaller pan and cut into ½-inch cubes. Set aside.

5. To make the topping: Scatter the marshmallows over the top of the cooled brownies in the larger pan.

6. Heat the butter, cocoa, and milk in a medium saucepan over medium heat, stirring, until the butter is melted. Whisk in the confectioners' sugar, and then stir in the vanilla. Pour the frosting evenly over the marshmallows. Sprinkle the reserved brownie cubes over the top.

7. Allow the topping to cool completely before cutting the brownies into 20 pieces. Store in an airtight container for up to 3 days.

Gooey Butter Bars

I arrived kind of late to the gooey-butter-bar party. It wasn't that long ago that I tasted my first such treat, but I was hooked immediately. I was at a cabin with my family, and my mom made a batch. We sat there and nibbled away at those bars until there were hardly any left. I just had to try out a red velvet version, and I'm so glad I did. These are delightful! MAKES 16

2 cups all-purpose flour

1½ cups granulated sugar

2 tablespoons natural unsweetened cocoa powder

2 teaspoons baking powder

½ teaspoon table salt

3 large eggs

1 cup (2 sticks) unsalted butter, melted

2 tablespoons buttermilk

1 tablespoon red liquid food coloring

8 ounces cream cheese, softened

1 teaspoon vanilla extract

4 cups confectioners' sugar, plus extra for dusting

1. Preheat the oven to 350°F. Spray a 9 x 13-inch baking dish with nonstick cooking spray.

2. Whisk the flour, granulated sugar, cocoa powder, baking powder, and salt in a large bowl to combine. Add 1 egg, ½ cup of the melted butter, the buttermilk, and the red food coloring. Mix to form a dough. Press into the bottom of the baking dish.

3. Beat the cream cheese in a large bowl with an electric mixer until smooth. Beat in the remaining 2 eggs, the vanilla, and the remaining ½ cup melted butter. Add the confectioners' sugar and beat until the mixture is creamy. Pour over the crust.

4. Bake for about 40 minutes, being careful not to overbake. The center should still be a little bit gooey. Cool completely. Dust with confectioners' sugar, then cut into 16 bars. Store in the refrigerator.

Seven-Layer Bars

These bars—also known as magic bars—are sweet, rich, and super easy to put together. A red velvet base is layered with a variety of toppings to create an addictive, crowd-pleasing bar. Bring these along to your next potluck and watch them disappear! MAKES 32

1¼ cups all-purpose flour
1 tablespoon natural unsweetened cocoa powder
½ teaspoon baking powder
⅛ teaspoon table salt
1 large egg
½ teaspoon vanilla extract
1 tablespoon red liquid food coloring
¾ cup sugar
8 tablespoons (1 stick) unsalted butter, softened
1⅓ cups sweetened shredded coconut
½ cup semisweet chocolate chips
½ cup milk chocolate chips
½ cup white chocolate chips
1 (14-ounce) can sweetened condensed milk
1 cup pecans, chopped

1. Set a rack in the center position and preheat the oven to 350°F. Spray a 9 x 13-inch baking dish with nonstick cooking spray.

2. Whisk the flour, cocoa, baking powder, and salt in a bowl to combine. Beat the egg, vanilla, and food coloring in a small bowl with a fork.

3. Beat the sugar and butter in a large bowl with an electric mixer until fluffy. Stir in the dry ingredients, then stir in the egg mixture. Press the dough into the bottom of the pan. Bake for 8 minutes. Remove the pan from the oven. Leave the oven on.

4. Sprinkle the coconut over the cookie layer, followed by the semisweet chocolate chips, milk chocolate chips, and white chocolate chips. Pour the sweetened condensed milk evenly over the top. Sprinkle on the pecans. Bake until set, about 25 minutes. Cool on a rack before slicing into 32 bars. Store in an airtight container for up to 3 days.

Shortbread Bars

Simplicity is part of shortbread's charm. These bars would fit in perfectly on a cookie platter, but they're also delightful on their own, as an afternoon snack. These keep well. **MAKES 12**

2 cups all-purpose flour
2 tablespoons natural unsweetened cocoa powder
¼ teaspoon baking powder
¼ teaspoon table salt
1 cup (2 sticks) unsalted butter, softened
½ cup confectioners' sugar, plus more for dusting
1 tablespoon red liquid food coloring

1. Set a rack in the center position and preheat the oven to 350°F.

2. Whisk the flour, cocoa, baking powder, and salt in a bowl to combine.

3. Beat the butter and ½ cup confectioners' sugar in a bowl with an electric mixer until fluffy. Beat in the food coloring. Add the dry ingredients and mix well.

4. Press the dough into an ungreased 7 x 11-inch baking pan. Prick with a fork. Bake until the edges start to brown, 20 to 25 minutes.

5. Cool on a rack, then dust with confectioners' sugar. Cut into 12 bars. Store in an airtight container for up to 1 month.

Breads

Red Velvet Bread

Each year, I do a week of red velvet recipes on my blog. One year, while brainstorming, the idea of a red velvet yeast bread popped into my head, and I knew I had to test it. At first I just used the dough to make Breakfast Rolls with Cream Cheese Icing (page 94), but I quickly realized how versatile this dough is. It bakes into a lovely loaf—and a slice, toasted and buttered, is one of my favorites.

MAKES 2 LOAVES

1½ cups buttermilk

8 tablespoons (1 stick) unsalted butter, cut in pieces

2 tablespoons red liquid food coloring

½ cup warm water

2 (¼-ounce) packages active dry yeast

½ cup sugar, plus an additional pinch

2 teaspoons table salt

½ teaspoon baking soda

¼ cup natural unsweetened cocoa powder

5 cups bread flour

1. Heat the buttermilk and butter in a medium saucepan over medium heat until the butter is melted. Remove from the heat and cool the mixture to lukewarm. Stir in the red food coloring.

2. Combine the warm water, yeast, and pinch of sugar in a small bowl and let sit until creamy, 5 to 10 minutes.

3. Combine the buttermilk mixture and the yeast mixture in the bowl of a stand mixer fitted with the paddle. Mix in the ½ cup sugar, the salt, and baking soda. Mix in the cocoa and 2 cups of the flour. Switch to the dough hook and continue adding flour, ½ cup at a time, until the dough starts to pull away from the sides of the bowl. (You may need a little more or a little less flour.) Knead at medium-low speed until the dough is smooth and tacky but not sticky, 3 to 5 minutes.

4. Oil a large bowl with vegetable oil. Turn the dough out onto a counter or work surface and form it into a ball. Put the dough into the bowl, then turn it over so the top is coated with oil. Cover the bowl with plastic wrap and allow the dough to rise in a warm spot until doubled in size, about 1½ hours.

5. Spray two 4 x 8-inch loaf pans with nonstick cooking spray.

RECIPE CONTINUES

6. Gently punch down the dough and divide it in half. Roll one portion of the dough into a large rectangle, about 8 x 16 inches. Roll up and place in a prepared loaf pan. Repeat with the remaining dough. Cover the pans with plastic wrap and allow the dough to rise in a warm spot until doubled in size, about 1 hour.

7. About 15 minutes before the loaves finish rising, set a rack in the center position and preheat the oven to 375°F. When rising is complete, bake the loaves until browned on top and cooked through, 30 to 35 minutes. Turn the loaves out to cool completely on a rack. Once cool, store in a plastic bread bag or an airtight container for up to 3 days.

RED VELVET BREAD, *variation*

Bread Pudding

I am all about not wasting any food at home. Bread pudding is one of those magic dishes that no one realizes is made from leftovers. But sometimes I'll make an extra loaf of bread just so I can prepare this for my husband. It's one of his favorite desserts.

Cut 1 loaf of Red Velvet Bread into 1-inch slices, then into 1-inch cubes. Place the cubes in a 9 x 13-inch baking dish sprayed with non-stick baking spray.

Whisk 3 cups half-and-half, 3 large eggs, and 1 large egg yolk in a large bowl to combine. Whisk in 1 teaspoon vanilla extract and a pinch of table salt.

Beat 8 ounces softened cream cheese and ¾ cup confectioners' sugar in a separate bowl with an electric mixer until light. Whisk the cream cheese mixture into the egg mixture. Pour the custard over the cubed bread, making sure to coat all of the bread in the custard.

Bake in the center of a preheated 350°F oven until the top springs back when lightly pressed, about 30 minutes. Dust the top of the bread pudding with additional confectioners' sugar. Serve warm.

OPPOSITE: Red Velvet Bread

Cocoa Rolls

Who doesn't love waking up to fresh-from-the-oven rolls? For this variation, think cinnamon rolls, but with a beautiful red velvet dough and cocoa in place of cinnamon. Make this recipe when you want something extra special—and extra delicious! MAKES 24

FOR THE ROLLS
¾ cup sugar
1 tablespoon natural unsweetened cocoa powder
1 batch of Red Velvet Bread dough (page 87), prepared through step 4
4 tablespoons (½ stick) unsalted butter, melted

FOR THE CREAM CHEESE FROSTING
8 ounces cream cheese, softened
8 tablespoons (1 stick) unsalted butter, softened
2 cups confectioners' sugar
½ teaspoon vanilla extract
1 to 2 tablespoons milk

1. To make the rolls: Spray two 9 x 13-inch baking dishes with nonstick cooking spray. Stir the sugar and cocoa together in a small bowl.

2. Gently punch down the dough and divide it in half. Roll one portion of the dough into a 12 x 16-inch rectangle. Brush half of the melted butter over the dough. Sprinkle half of the sugar mixture evenly over the dough.

3. Starting on the long side, roll the dough into a log. Cut the dough into 12 equal slices. Place the slices, cut side up, in one of the baking dishes. Repeat with the remaining dough. Cover both dishes with plastic wrap and allow the rolls to rise in a warm spot until doubled, about 1 hour.

4. About 15 minutes before the rolls finish rising, preheat the oven to 350°F. When the rising is complete, bake the rolls until the tops are golden, about 20 minutes. Cool on racks for about 10 minutes.

5. To make the frosting: Beat the cream cheese and butter in a large bowl with an electric mixer until light and fluffy. Beat in the confectioners' sugar. Beat in the vanilla and 1 tablespoon of milk. Beat in more milk if needed to make a spreadable consistency. Spread the frosting over the warm rolls.

6. Serve warm or at room temperature. Cover leftovers with plastic wrap and store in the refrigerator for up to 2 days.

Pull-Apart Bread

I adore monkey bread, but I think I like pull-apart bread even more! If you've never had pull-apart bread, just imagine pulling pieces of gooey red velvet bread from a loaf—no knife required. Make sure you chop the white chocolate chips so they don't sink to the bottom of the bread. The glaze takes this treat over the top!

This can easily be made into mini loaves—perfect for gift giving. **MAKES 2 LOAVES**

FOR THE BREAD
1 batch of Red Velvet Bread dough (page 87), prepared through step 4
3 tablespoons unsalted butter, softened
½ cup sugar
½ cup white chocolate chips, coarsely chopped

FOR THE GLAZE
4 ounces cream cheese, softened
¾ cup confectioners' sugar
1 tablespoon unsalted butter, softened
3 tablespoons milk

1. To make the bread: Spray two 4 x 8-inch loaf pans with nonstick cooking spray.

2. Divide the dough in half. Roll one half of the dough into a 12 x 15-inch rectangle. Brush the dough with half of the softened butter. Sprinkle with half of the sugar and chocolate chips, pressing them lightly into the dough. Slice the dough into 6 strips (each 2 x 15 inches), stack the strips, and cut each stacked strip into 6 pieces. Set the stacks upright, side by side, in one of the loaf pans. Repeat with the remaining dough and ingredients. Cover the pans with plastic wrap and allow the loaves to rise in a warm spot until doubled, about 1 hour.

3. About 15 minutes before the loaves finish rising, preheat the oven to 350°F. When the rising is complete, bake the loaves until golden brown, 30 to 35 minutes. Cool on racks.

4. To make the glaze: Beat the cream cheese, confectioners' sugar, and butter in a mixing bowl with an electric mixer until light and fluffy. Beat in the milk, 1 tablespoon at a time, until the mixture reaches a drizzling consistency. Remove the loaves from the pans and drizzle with the glaze. Cover with plastic wrap and store in the refrigerator for up to 2 days.

Breakfast Rolls with Cream Cheese Icing

Not all rolls are made for the dinner table. These rolls are just slightly sweet and make a perfect addition to a birthday breakfast or brunch. They can be served with or without the cream cheese icing, but I definitely like them with! MAKES 24

1 batch of Red Velvet Bread dough (page 87), prepared through step 4
8 ounces cream cheese, softened
1 cup confectioners' sugar
2 teaspoons vanilla extract
⅓ cup milk

1. Spray two 12-cavity muffin tins with nonstick cooking spray.

2. Punch down dough. Pinch off about 1 tablespoon of dough and roll it into a ball. Place 3 balls into each muffin tin. Cover with plastic wrap and allow the rolls to rise in a warm spot until doubled, about 1 hour.

3. About 15 minutes before the rolls have finished rising, preheat the oven to 350°F. When the rising is complete, bake the rolls until cooked through, about 20 minutes. Remove the rolls from the pans and place on racks to cool completely.

4. Beat the cream cheese, confectioners' sugar, and vanilla in a mixing bowl with an electric mixer until light and fluffy. Beat in the milk, 1 tablespoon at a time, until the glaze is thin enough to drizzle. Drizzle the glaze over the rolls and allow it to set before serving. Store in an airtight container in the refrigerator for up to 2 days.

Ice Cream
AND Frozen
Desserts

Cheesecake and Red Velvet Cake Ice Cream

When you mix homemade cheesecake ice cream with red velvet cake chunks, you make what may be the perfect frozen treat. I can't resist going back to the freezer with a spoon multiple times for "just one more bite"! **MAKES 1½ QUARTS**

FOR THE CAKE

1⅛ cups all-purpose flour

1 tablespoon natural unsweetened cocoa powder

½ teaspoon table salt

4 tablespoons (½ stick) unsalted butter, softened

¾ cup sugar

1 large egg

½ cup buttermilk

1½ tablespoons red liquid food coloring

½ teaspoon vanilla extract

½ teaspoon distilled white vinegar

½ teaspoon baking soda

FOR THE CHEESECAKE ICE CREAM

1 cup sugar

3 ounces cream cheese, softened

2 large egg yolks

1 cup milk

1 cup heavy cream

1. To make the cake: Set a rack in the center position and preheat the oven to 350°F. Spray a 9 x 13-inch rimmed baking sheet with non-stick cooking spray.

2. Whisk the flour, cocoa, and salt in a bowl to combine. Beat the butter and sugar in a large bowl with an electric mixer until fluffy, about 5 minutes. Beat in the egg, then scrape down the sides of the bowl. Add the dry ingredients and the buttermilk to the creamed butter and sugar in two or three alternating additions, mixing until combined. Stir in the red food coloring and vanilla.

3. Stir the vinegar and baking soda together in a small bowl (it will bubble up). Fold into the cake batter. Pour the batter onto the baking sheet and spread it out evenly. Bake until the cake springs back when lightly touched, about 15 minutes. Let the cake cool completely in the pan. Cut half of the cake into ½-inch squares, reserving the remaining cake for another use.

RECIPE CONTINUES

4. To make the cheesecake ice cream: Fill a large bowl with ice water. Beat the sugar, cream cheese, and egg yolks in a large bowl with an electric mixer until fluffy.

5. Bring the milk and heavy cream to a simmer in a saucepan over medium heat. Beat half of the hot milk mixture into the sugar mixture, then pour this mixture back into the saucepan. Cook over medium-low heat, stirring constantly, until the custard thickens, about 5 minutes. Pour the custard into a bowl and place the bowl in the ice water to cool the custard quickly, stirring it occasionally. When the custard is cool, cover it with plastic wrap and refrigerate until completely cold.

6. Place the custard in an ice cream maker and churn according to the manufacturer's instructions. When the ice cream is finished churning, gently stir in the cake pieces. Transfer to a plastic container and freeze for at least 2 hours before serving.

CHEESECAKE AND RED VELVET CAKE ICE CREAM, *variation*

Red Velvet Cake Milk Shakes

For each milk shake, combine 1 cup Cheesecake and Red Velvet Cake Ice Cream and ½ cup milk in a blender and blend until smooth. Pour into a large glass. Sprinkle more pieces of cake on top, if desired.

OPPOSITE:
Cheesecake and Red Velvet Cake Ice Cream

Frozen Cheesecake Pie

Summer's the time for no-bake frozen desserts. This pie is easy as can be and pretty enough to serve to guests. Make sure you use a deep-dish pie plate, because there's too much filling for a standard pie plate. And it would be naughty if you just ate the leftover filling with a spoon, right?

MAKES ONE 9-INCH PIE

FOR THE CRUST
24 chocolate sandwich cookies
4 tablespoons (½ stick) unsalted butter, melted

FOR THE FILLING
2 tablespoons red liquid food coloring
1 tablespoon natural unsweetened cocoa powder
8 ounces cream cheese, softened
1 (14-ounce) can sweetened condensed milk
1¼ cups heavy cream
2 tablespoons confectioners' sugar

1. To make the crust: Place the cookies in a food processor and pulse until they are fine crumbs. Combine the crumbs with the melted butter and press the mixture into the bottom of a 9-inch deep-dish pie plate. Refrigerate for 1 hour.

2. To make the filling: Stir the food coloring and cocoa together in a small bowl to make a smooth paste. Beat the cream cheese and sweetened condensed milk in a large bowl with an electric mixer until smooth. Beat in the dissolved cocoa.

3. Whip ¾ cup of the cream with an electric mixer in a mixing bowl until stiff peaks form. Fold the whipped cream into the cream cheese mixture. Pour the mixture into the cookie crust.

4. Cover the pie with plastic wrap and freeze until completely frozen, 6 to 8 hours.

5. Whip the remaining ½ cup cream and confectioners' sugar until stiff peaks form. Serve each slice of the frozen pie with a dollop of the whipped cream.

Baked Alaska

This dessert appears a lot more complicated than it really is, and that will make you look like a kitchen superstar to your dinner guests. It's also perfect for entertaining, because the majority of the work is done ahead of time. Prepare it earlier in the day and freeze it until right before you are ready to serve dessert. You can stick it in the oven to brown the meringue or, even more impressive, whip out the kitchen torch and brown the meringue in front of your guests!

This dessert will take up quite a bit of your freezer space, so make sure you have room before you start. Note, too, that the dish requires 10 hours total freezing time, so plan accordingly.

MAKES ONE 9-INCH DESSERT

1¾ quarts (7 cups) vanilla ice cream, softened

FOR THE CAKE
1⅛ cups all-purpose flour
1 tablespoon natural unsweetened cocoa powder
½ teaspoon table salt
4 tablespoons (½ stick) unsalted butter, softened
¾ cup sugar
1 large egg
½ cup buttermilk
2 tablespoons red liquid food coloring
½ teaspoon vanilla extract
½ teaspoon distilled white vinegar
½ teaspoon baking soda

FOR THE MERINGUE
6 large egg whites
½ teaspoon cream of tartar
⅛ teaspoon table salt
¾ cup sugar

1. Line a 9-inch-diameter bowl with plastic wrap. Pack the ice cream into the bowl, smoothing the top with an offset spatula. Cover the bowl with plastic wrap and freeze until frozen solid, about 8 hours.

2. To make the cake: Preheat the oven to 350°F. Spray a 9-inch round cake pan with nonstick cooking spray. Line the pan with parchment paper and spray the paper.

3. Whisk the flour, cocoa, and salt in a bowl to combine.

4. Beat the butter and sugar in a large bowl with an electric mixer until fluffy. Beat in the egg, then scrape down the sides of the bowl. Add the dry ingredients and the buttermilk to the creamed butter and sugar in two or three alternating additions, mixing until combined. Stir in the red food coloring and vanilla.

RECIPE CONTINUES

5. Combine the vinegar and baking soda in a small bowl (it will bubble up). Fold into the cake batter. Pour the batter into the pan. Bake until the cake springs back when lightly touched, about 25 minutes. Let the cake cool for 10 minutes, then turn out onto a cooling rack to cool completely.

6. To make the meringue: Beat the egg whites with an electric mixer in a large bowl until frothy. Add the cream of tartar and salt and beat until soft peaks form. Gradually beat in the sugar and beat until stiff peaks form.

7. To assemble the dessert: If necessary, level off the top of the cake with a serrated knife. Place the cake layer on a parchment paper–lined baking sheet. Remove the plastic wrap covering the bowl of ice cream and unmold the ice cream, flat side down, on the cake layer. Peel the plastic wrap off the ice cream. Cover the cake and ice cream with the meringue, making sure to reach all the way down to the parchment paper, leaving no holes. Use the back of a spoon to make peaks in the meringue. Freeze the dessert for 2 hours.

8. When ready to serve, set a rack in the center position and preheat the oven to 425°F. Remove the dessert from the freezer and bake just until the meringue is browned, about 8 minutes. Alternatively, brown the meringue with a kitchen torch. Serve immediately.

OTHER
Indulgences

Red Velvet Truffles

These smooth red velvet truffles are rolled in cocoa powder for a special and impressive treat.

Making candy and chocolates can be a bit intimidating. But believe me when I say that preparing these homemade truffles is much easier than you'd expect. They make the perfect gift for someone you love! MAKES 24

6 ounces white chocolate, chopped
2 ounces semisweet chocolate, chopped
4 ounces cream cheese, softened
¼ cup confectioners' sugar
½ teaspoon red liquid food coloring
¼ cup natural unsweetened cocoa powder

1. Combine the white chocolate and semisweet chocolate in a microwave-safe bowl. Microwave on 50 percent power in 30-second increments, stirring after each increment, until melted.

2. Beat the cream cheese and confectioners' sugar with an electric mixer in a mixing bowl until fluffy. Beat in the food coloring. Beat in the melted chocolate mixture. Cover the bowl with plastic wrap and refrigerate until very firm, about 4 hours.

3. Roll the truffle mixture into 24 balls and place on a parchment paper–lined baking sheet. Refrigerate until solid, at least 1 hour.

4. Put the cocoa powder in a shallow dish. Roll each ball in the cocoa to coat completely, shaking off any excess. Store the truffles in the refrigerator.

Red Velvet–Filled Chocolate Cups

Could there be a more perfect Valentine's Day gift for a loved one? Chocolate may say "I love you," but homemade chocolate cups filled with red velvet cream cheese fairly scream it.

These cups need to be stored in the refrigerator but are best served at room temperature.

MAKES 24

2¼ cups semisweet chocolate chips
8 ounces cream cheese, softened
1½ cups confectioners' sugar
1 tablespoon red liquid food coloring
1 tablespoon milk
2 teaspoons natural unsweetened cocoa powder

1. Line a 24-cavity mini muffin tin with paper liners.

2. Melt 1¼ cups of the chocolate chips in the top of a double boiler. Working quickly, add about 1 teaspoon of the melted chocolate to each of the liners. Use a pastry brush or the back of a spoon to spread the chocolate evenly across the bottom and up the sides of the liners. Place in the freezer for 20 minutes for the chocolate to set.

3. Beat the cream cheese and confectioners' sugar in a medium bowl with an electric mixer until fluffy. Add the food coloring, milk, and cocoa and beat until smooth. Divide the mixture evenly among the 24 cups. Freeze for another 10 to 15 minutes.

4. Melt the remaining 1 cup chocolate chips in the top of a double boiler. Cover the top of each cup with the chocolate and use a spoon to smooth the top. Return to the freezer for another 20 minutes for the chocolate to set, then transfer to the refrigerator for storage.

5. Serve at room temperature.

Red Velvet Eclairs

If there is one thing my mom is known for, it's her éclairs. They are her most requested dessert—beloved by her family and by anyone who has had the opportunity to try them. Now, these are definitely not my mother's éclairs, but I think this fun version might come in second next to Mom's!

MAKES ABOUT 36

FOR THE PUDDING

1 cup milk

1 cup heavy cream

⅓ cup sugar

2 tablespoons cornstarch

1 tablespoon natural unsweetened cocoa powder

¼ teaspoon table salt

1 tablespoon red liquid food coloring

1 teaspoon vanilla extract

2 tablespoons unsalted butter, cut into small cubes

FOR THE ECLAIR SHELLS

8 tablespoons (1 stick) unsalted butter, cut into pieces

1 cup water

1 cup all-purpose flour

¼ teaspoon table salt

4 large eggs

FOR THE CHOCOLATE GLAZE

2 ounces semisweet chocolate, chopped

2 tablespoons unsalted butter

1 cup confectioners' sugar

1 teaspoon vanilla extract

3 tablespoons hot water

1. To make the pudding: Whisk the milk, cream, sugar, cornstarch, cocoa powder, and salt in a medium saucepan to combine. Cook over medium heat, whisking frequently, until the pudding starts to thicken. When the pudding comes to a boil, whisk it constantly until thickened. Remove from the heat and whisk in the food coloring and vanilla. Add the butter and stir until the butter is melted. Transfer the pudding to a bowl and press a piece of plastic wrap directly onto the surface of the pudding. Refrigerate until it is set, 4 hours to overnight.

2. To make the éclair shells: Position oven racks in the upper and lower thirds of the oven and preheat the oven to 450°F. Line two baking sheets with parchment paper.

3. Place the butter and water in a saucepan over medium heat. Bring to a boil. When the butter is melted, reduce the heat to low and add the flour and salt, stirring with a wooden spoon until the mixture forms a ball. Remove from the heat. Beat in the eggs with a wooden spoon or electric mixer, one at a time, making sure each egg is completely incorporated before adding the next one.

4. Transfer the dough to a pastry bag fitted with a plain tip with a ⅓- to ½-inch opening. Pipe 2-inch lengths of dough onto the lined baking sheets, leaving 2 inches between each length of dough. Bake for 15 minutes, switch the pans from top to bottom, then reduce the heat to 325°F and bake until golden brown and cooked through, about 15 minutes. Cool completely on racks.

5. When the éclair shells are cool, slice off the tops lengthwise. Spoon the pudding inside the shell and replace the tops.

6. To make the chocolate glaze: Cook the chocolate and butter in a small saucepan over low heat until melted. Remove from the heat and whisk in the confectioners' sugar until smooth, then whisk in the vanilla and hot water.

7. Frost the top of each éclair with the chocolate glaze. Chill for 1 hour to let the glaze set. Serve chilled. Store the éclairs covered in the refrigerator for up to 3 days.

Pots de Crème

The name might sound fancy, but these are really just simple custards—with that red velvet touch. Creamy and decadent, these would be a great way to finish off any dinner. **MAKES 6**

1½ cups heavy cream
½ cup milk
5 large egg yolks
¼ cup sugar
1 tablespoon red liquid food coloring
A pinch of table salt
1 ounce semisweet chocolate, melted
Whipped cream, for serving (optional)

1. Set a rack in the center position and preheat the oven to 375°F. Place a kitchen towel in a 9 x 13-inch casserole dish. Place six ¾-cup ramekins on top of the towel.

2. Bring the cream and milk to a simmer in a saucepan.

3. Whisk the egg yolks, sugar, food coloring, and salt in a large bowl until the sugar is dissolved. Slowly whisk in the milk and cream, then slowly whisk in the chocolate. Ladle the mixture evenly into the ramekins.

4. Place the baking dish in the oven and add enough hot or boiling water to come halfway up the sides of the ramekins. Bake until set around the edges, about 35 minutes.

5. Lift the ramekins out of the dish with tongs and place on a rack until cool enough to handle. Cover with plastic wrap and chill thoroughly in the refrigerator. Serve cold with whipped cream, if desired.

Funnel Cake

A trip to the fair is not complete without funnel cake. But now you can have your funnel cake at home—red velvet style! These are wonderful served with just a dusting of powdered sugar, but if you want to go all out, top them with whipped cream and berries. **SERVES 4**

Vegetable oil for frying
1 tablespoon red liquid food coloring
2 teaspoons natural unsweetened cocoa powder
1 large egg
⅔ cup milk
1¼ cups all-purpose flour
2 tablespoons sugar
1 teaspoon baking powder
¼ teaspoon table salt
Confectioners' sugar
Whipped cream and berries, for serving (optional)

1. Fill a Dutch oven or heavy–bottomed pot with oil to a depth of about 2 inches and heat to 350°F.

2. Stir the food coloring and cocoa together in a small bowl to make a smooth paste.

3. Beat the egg and milk in a mixing bowl. Stir in the flour, sugar, baking powder, and salt. Stir in the dissolved cocoa.

4. Place the batter in a zip-top plastic bag and carefully snip off one corner. Starting from the center of the pan, use a swirling motion to drizzle batter into the oil, making a round about 6 inches in diameter. Fry, turning once, until golden brown on both sides, about 2 minutes per side. Drain on paper towels.

5. Serve topped with confectioners' sugar and, if desired, whipped cream and berries.

Red Velvet Cannoli

I hope to visit Italy one day and have real, authentic cannoli. But until then, I have these Red Velvet Cannoli to enjoy. These do require cannoli molds—stainless steel tubes that you use to form the cannoli shells. Luckily, they are pretty inexpensive. Many kitchen supply stores sell them, but if you can't find them locally, they are easy to locate online. Since you're cooking only 2 or 3 cannoli shells at a time, you need to purchase only 2 or 3 molds and reuse them to cook the entire batch. **MAKES ABOUT 12**

FOR THE FILLING

2 cups ricotta cheese
¾ cup confectioners' sugar
8 ounces cream cheese, softened
½ tablespoon vanilla extract
¼ cup miniature chocolate chips

FOR THE SHELLS

2 cups all-purpose flour
1 tablespoon sugar
1 teaspoon natural unsweetened cocoa powder
¼ teaspoon table salt
1½ tablespoons unsalted butter
1 large egg, separated
¼ cup plus 1 tablespoon water
1 tablespoon red liquid food coloring
Vegetable oil for frying

1. To make the filling: Line a colander with cheesecloth, put the ricotta in the colander, and set it on a plate in the refrigerator to drain until it is dry, a few hours to overnight.

2. Beat the drained ricotta, confectioners' sugar, cream cheese, and vanilla in a mixing bowl. Cover with plastic wrap and chill for 30 minutes.

3. To make the shells: Whisk the flour, sugar, cocoa, and salt in a large bowl to combine. Cut in the butter with a pastry cutter or a fork. Add the egg yolk and stir to combine. Combine the water and the food coloring and add to the flour mixture 1 tablespoon at a time, stirring until the dough comes together. Form the dough into a ball, cover it with a towel, and let it sit for 30 minutes.

4. Fill a Dutch oven or heavy-bottomed pot with oil to a depth of about 4 inches and heat to 375°F over medium-high heat. Beat the egg white lightly with a fork.

5. Roll the dough out on a floured surface to a thickness of about ⅛ inch. Using a cutter or the rim of a glass with a 3½-inch diameter, cut out circles of dough. Wrap the circles around the cannoli molds, brushing one end of each circle with egg white and pressing it firmly onto the opposite end to make a seal. Fry the shells in the hot oil, 2 or 3 at a time, until golden brown, 2 to 3 minutes. Turn with tongs if needed. Carefully remove and drain on a wire rack or on paper towels. Cool just enough to handle, then twist the tubes to remove them from the shell. Wash the tubes to use for the remaining dough circles.

6. To assemble the cannoli: Just before serving, put the chocolate chips in a shallow bowl. Transfer the filling to a pastry bag fitted with a large star tip. Pipe the filling into the shells from both sides. Dip the ends in the chocolate chips. The unfilled cannoli shells can be stored in an airtight container for 3 to 4 days. Once filled, serve the cannoli immediately, as they do not store well.

Churros and Hot Chocolate

I'm a donut lover, so it probably comes as no surprise that I also love churros—those fried pastries sometimes called Spanish donuts. There's just something about deep-fried dough that I can't get enough of. These are perfect for a cold day—served alongside a warm mug of red velvet hot chocolate. Snow falling outside and a fire in the fireplace are optional! **SERVES 4**

FOR THE COATING
½ cup sugar
1 teaspoon ground cinnamon

FOR THE CHURROS
Vegetable oil for frying, plus 2 tablespoons
1 cup all-purpose flour
2 teaspoons natural unsweetened cocoa powder
1 cup water
2½ tablespoons sugar
1 tablespoon red liquid food coloring
½ teaspoon table salt

FOR THE HOT CHOCOLATE
6 cups milk
1 cup plus 2 tablespoons milk chocolate chips
6 tablespoons white chocolate chips
3 teaspoons red liquid food coloring

1. To make the coating: Whisk the sugar and cinnamon in a shallow bowl to combine. Set aside.

2. To make the churros: Fill a Dutch oven or heavy-bottomed pot with oil to a depth of several inches and heat to 375°F over medium-high heat.

3. Whisk the flour and cocoa together.

4. Bring the water, sugar, food coloring, salt, and 2 tablespoons vegetable oil to a boil in a medium saucepan, then remove from the heat. Add the dry ingredients and stir until the batter forms a ball.

5. To make the hot chocolate: Heat the milk in a saucepan over medium heat until it simmers. Remove from the heat and add the milk chocolate chips and the white chocolate chips. Whisk until the chips have melted. Whisk in the food coloring. Keep warm on very low heat while you cook the churros.

6. To fry the churros, transfer the batter to a pastry bag fitted with a large star tip. Pipe strips of batter into the hot oil and fry until golden brown, 3 to 4 minutes. Drain on paper towels.

7. While they're still hot, roll the churros in the coating. Place on a serving dish and serve immediately, accompanied by hot chocolate.

Red Velvet "Twinkies"

When I was growing up, I was only allowed store-bought treats when we went camping in the summer. To this day, I think of Twinkies and crème-filled cupcakes as camping delicacies. Thank goodness I can make them at home from scratch now—campfire optional!

This recipe calls for a specialty pan called a cream canoe pan. You will need two, and you can find them at kitchen supply stores or online. If you don't want to make the investment, you can make your own version using tin foil formed around a spice bottle. Remove the spice bottle, place the mold on a pan, and you have a way to make "Twinkies" without any specialty equipment!

You will also need a pastry bag with an Ateco Bismark #230 decorating tip. **MAKES 12**

FOR THE CAKES

¾ cup all-purpose flour
1 tablespoon cornstarch
2 teaspoons natural unsweetened cocoa powder
¾ teaspoon baking powder
A pinch of table salt
3 large eggs, separated
3 tablespoons water
¾ cup sugar
¼ cup vegetable oil
1 tablespoon red liquid food coloring
1 teaspoon vanilla extract

FOR THE FILLING

1 (7-ounce) container marshmallow crème
½ cup shortening
⅓ cup confectioners' sugar
1 teaspoon water
½ teaspoon vanilla extract

1. To make the cakes: Set a rack in the center position and preheat the oven to 350°F. Spray 12 cavities in the cream canoe pans with non-stick cooking spray.

2. Whisk the flour, cornstarch, cocoa powder, baking powder, and salt in a bowl to combine. Beat the egg whites with an electric mixer in a large bowl until stiff peaks form; set aside.

3. Beat the egg yolks in a large bowl with an electric mixer until very light in color, about 5 minutes. Add the water, sugar, vegetable oil, food coloring, and vanilla and beat to combine. Stir in the dry ingredients. Fold in the egg whites.

4. Fill the molds about two-thirds full with batter. Bake until a toothpick inserted in the center comes out clean, about 30 minutes. Let the cakes cool for a few minutes in the pan, then remove them to racks to cool completely.

5. To make the filling: Beat the marshmallow crème, shortening, confectioners' sugar, water, and vanilla in a large bowl with an electric mixer until light and fluffy. Transfer the filling to a pastry bag fitted with an Ateco #230 tip. Poke the tip into the bottom of a cake, near one end. Carefully pipe in filling until you feel the cake expand, but do not overfill, which would cause the cake to crack. Repeat in the center of the cake and at the other end. Fill the rest of the cakes. Store in an airtight container for up to 3 days.

Red Velvet Trifle

I have a fabulous group of foodie friends, and one day we were all getting together for a potluck lunch. I brought this trifle, and it was a hit. If a group of foodies approves, you know you have a winner!

SERVES 8 TO 10

FOR THE CAKE
2¼ cups all-purpose flour
2 tablespoons natural unsweetened cocoa powder
1 teaspoon table salt
8 tablespoons (1 stick) unsalted butter, softened
1½ cups sugar
2 large eggs
1 cup buttermilk
4 tablespoons red liquid food coloring
1 teaspoon vanilla extract
1 teaspoon distilled white vinegar
1 teaspoon baking soda

FOR THE FILLING
2 (8-ounce) packages cream cheese, softened
2 cups vanilla yogurt
1 cup confectioners' sugar
1 teaspoon grated lemon zest

FOR ASSEMBLY
2 pounds fresh strawberries, hulled and sliced

1. To make the cake: Set a rack in the center position and preheat the oven to 350°F. Spray a 9 x 13-inch baking dish with nonstick cooking spray.

2. Whisk the flour, cocoa, and salt in a bowl to combine.

3. Beat the butter and sugar in a large bowl with an electric mixer until fluffy. Beat in the eggs, one at a time, scraping down the sides of the bowl between additions. Add the dry ingredients and the buttermilk to the creamed butter and sugar mixture in two or three alternating additions, mixing until combined. Mix in the food coloring and vanilla.

4. Combine the vinegar and baking soda in a small bowl (it will bubble up). Fold into the batter.

5. Spread the batter evenly in the baking dish and bake until the cake springs back when lightly touched, 30 to 35 minutes. Let the cake cool completely on a rack.

6. To make the filling: Beat the cream cheese in a large bowl with an electric mixer until smooth. Add the yogurt, confectioners' sugar, and lemon zest and beat until smooth. Cover with plastic wrap and refrigerate until set, about 1 hour.

7. To assemble the trifle: Cut the cake into 1-inch squares. Put one-third of the cake squares in the bottom of a trifle dish. Spread one-third of the filling over the cake, then scatter one-third of the sliced strawberries over the filling. Repeat the layers two more times, ending with strawberries on top. Cover with plastic wrap and refrigerate for 1 hour before serving.

Acknowledgments

I remember sitting at my desk at my office job years ago, daydreaming. I was thinking about how awesome it would be if I could just blog full-time—spend my days in the kitchen, creating and photographing, doing what I loved to do. I still have to pinch myself sometimes, now that that dream has come true. Thank you so much to the readers of Taste and Tell for coming back again and again and for reading my blog and making my recipes. None of this would have been possible without you!

Thank you to The Harvard Common Press and to Dan Rosenberg, for sending that email that I never thought I would receive from a publishing company. Thank you for testing my creativity and for believing in me from the beginning. Thank you to Virginia Downes for helping me break out of my comfort zone for the photography for this book. And thanks to all the editors and other people who helped to bring this book to life. I never realized what a village it takes, and I'm honored to have worked with such an amazing village.

Thank you to my sisters and sister-in-law, for brainstorming with me to come up with countless recipe ideas for this book. You all helped me when I thought I had already thought of it all. To my mom, who gave me my love of cooking and baking: Thank you for cooking for your family three times a day when I was growing up, teaching me the value and joy you get from a home-cooked meal. Thank you to my dad, for always believing in me and telling me how proud you are of me, and to my brother for taste testing and giving me such great advice.

Thank you to my Utah food blogging community. You all have helped me grow so much as a blogger and as a cook, and I will forever be indebted to you for your advice and support. Thanks to Carrian and Kristy for always being there for me and becoming two of my best friends, and to Heidi for your endless advice and inspiration.

And most of all, thank you to my forever companion, Josh, and my three beautiful children, Abigail, Easton, and Camden. You all have stuck with me through the good times and the bad, and have always supported me and encouraged me. Thank you, Josh, for always believing in me and for being my biggest cheerleader. Thank you for your honest opinions and your honest praise. I love you forever.

Measurement Equivalents

Please note that all conversions are approximate.

Liquid Conversions

U.S.	Metric
1 tsp	5 ml
1 tbs	15 ml
2 tbs	30 ml
3 tbs	45 ml
¼ cup	60 ml
⅓ cup	75 ml
⅓ cup + 1 tbs	90 ml
⅓ cup + 2 tbs	100 ml
½ cup	120 ml
⅔ cup	150 ml
¾ cup	180 ml
¾ cup + 2 tbs	200 ml
1 cup	240 ml
1 cup + 2 tbs	275 ml
1¼ cups	300 ml
1⅓ cups	325 ml
1½ cups	350 ml
1⅔ cups	375 ml
1¾ cups	400 ml
1¾ cups + 2 tbs	450 ml
2 cups (1 pint)	475 ml
2½ cups	600 ml
3 cups	720 ml
4 cups (1 quart)	945 ml
(1,000 ml is 1 liter)	

Weight Conversions

U.S./U.K.	Metric
½ oz	14 g
1 oz	28 g
1½ oz	43 g
2 oz	57 g
2½ oz	71 g
3 oz	85 g
3½ oz	100 g
4 oz	113 g
5 oz	142 g
6 oz	170 g
7 oz	200 g
8 oz	227 g
9 oz	255 g
10 oz	284 g
11 oz	312 g
12 oz	340 g
13 oz	368 g
14 oz	400 g
15 oz	425 g
1 lb	454 g

Oven Temperature Conversions

°F	Gas Mark	°C
250	½	120
275	1	140
300	2	150
325	3	165
350	4	180
375	5	190
400	6	200
425	7	220
450	8	230
475	9	240
500	10	260
550	Broil	290

Index

W

Waffles, Red Velvet, 28

White Chocolate. *See also* White Chocolate
    Chips
    Cream Cheese Frosting, 17
    Molten Lava Cakes, 53
    Red Velvet Biscotti, 72
    Red Velvet Truffles, 106

White Chocolate Chips
    Cookie Mix in a Jar, 61
    Cookies with, 65
    Hot Chocolate, 119
    Pull-Apart Bread, 93
    Seven-Layer Bars, 82

Whoopie Pies, 66–67

Y

Yogurt
    Red Velvet Trifle, 122–23

About the Author

Deborah Harroun's blog, Taste and Tell, has attracted a large and loyal following since she launched it in 2007. In it she writes about family-friendly food, with an emphasis on ease and speed of preparation. Her desserts and sweets are especially popular with her readers, and she was among the first food writers and bloggers to identify the red velvet trend and to create new recipes to feed the growing interest in the topic. Her recipes and writing have been featured or excerpted in numerous places in print and online, including *Every Day with Rachael Ray*, *Bon Appétit*, iVillage, *Better Homes & Gardens*, Babble, The Kitchn, and Huffington Post. She lives with her husband and three young children in the Salt Lake City area, where she appears frequently as a cooking authority on local television news and lifestyle shows.